Simple
Sermons
on
CONVERSION
and
commitment

THE "SIMPLE SERMON" SERIES BY W. HERSCHEL FORD . . .

Seven Simple Sermons on the Saviour's Last Words
Seven Simple Sermons on the Second Coming
Simple Sermons About Jesus Christ
Simple Sermons for a Sinful Age
Simple Sermons for Funeral Services
Simple Sermons for Midweek Services
Simple Sermons for Saints and Sinners
Simple Sermons for Special Days and Occasions
Simple Sermons for Sunday Evening
Simple Sermons for Sunday Morning
Simple Sermons for Time and Eternity
Simple Sermons for Times Like These
Simple Sermons for Today's World
Simple Sermons for 20th Century Christians
Simple Sermons on Conversion and Commitment
Simple Sermons From the Book of Acts
Simple Sermons From the Gospel of John
Simple Sermons From the Gospel of Matthew
Simple Sermons on Evangelistic Themes
Simple Sermons on Heaven, Hell and Judgment
Simple Sermons on Prayer
Simple Sermons on Prophetic Themes
Simple Sermons on Salvation and Service
Simple Sermons on Simple Themes
Simple Sermons on the Christian Life
Simple Sermons on Great Christian Doctrines
Simple Sermons on the Old-Time Religion
Simple Sermons on the Seven Churches of Revelation
Simple Sermons on the Ten Commandments
Simple Talks for Christian Workers
Simple Sermons on Life and Living
Simple Sermons for Modern Man
Simple Sermons on Old Testament Texts
Simple Sermons on New Testament Texts
Simple Sermons for a World in Crisis
Simple Sermons on Grace and Glory

Simple Sermons on Conversion and Commitment

by
W. HERSCHEL FORD

ZONDERVAN PUBLISHING HOUSE
OF THE ZONDERVAN CORPORATION
GRAND RAPIDS, MICHIGAN 49506

SIMPLE SERMONS ON CONVERSION AND COMMITMENT
Copyright © 1972 by The Zondervan Corporation
Grand Rapids, Michigan

Seventh printing 1979

ISBN 0-310-24441-2

Library of Congress Catalog Card Number 76-189575

Printed in the United States of America

Contents

Foreword

Because of the reception given my other "Simple Sermon" books, I am now sending out this volume entitled, *Simple Sermons on Conversion and Commitment.*

There are two sides to the Christian life. First, there must be conversion, a saving experience with Jesus Christ. Second, there should be a growth in grace until the day the Lord takes us home. In these sermons I have sought to cover both of these phases.

My preacher brethren and all Christian workers are certainly free to use anything in these sermons for the glory of God, the upbuilding of Christians, and the salvation of souls.

W. Herschel Ford

1

SIXTY SECONDS AFTER SALVATION

John 6:35-40

When I was still a teen-age boy I left the little town where I was born and went to the big city to seek a job. In the city I found a room with a nice family. They had something in their home which I had never seen before. It was an instantaneous gas water heater. You would first light the gas jet, then, by the time you turned on the water, it would be getting hot. The heating process was indeed swift.

Now salvation is like that. Jesus assures us that we are saved the instant we come to Him in saving faith. We cease to be the children of Satan and we become the children of God. Our names are written down in the Lamb's Book of Life and we are on our way to heaven. It is an instantaneous change. When a baby is born into the world, all of its surroundings are strange and new. Doctors tell us that there are fifty or sixty changes that take place in a new-born babe in the first few seconds of life. And when a person is born spiritually through the new birth, many changes take place immediately.

Let us think of some things that happen sixty seconds after salvation.

I. SIXTY SECONDS AFTER SALVATION WE WANT THE WORLD TO KNOW IT

Take the case of Andrew. Always we see him as a quiet and reserved man. But as soon as he met Jesus he ran

9

home to tell his brother, Simon Peter, of his wonderful discovery and experience. And then there follows an account of the greatest thing one person can do for another. "And he brought him to Jesus" (John 1:42). That is the natural reaction of every new-born Christian. This is one of the evidences that a man truly has been saved.

Jesus tells us that if we confess Him before men He will confess us before the Father in heaven.

Let us contrast the attitude of two people mentioned in the Book of John. Nicodemus came to Jesus by night and heard His great message on the new birth. Did he receive Jesus as his personal Saviour? We hope he did, but the Bible doesn't tell us that he did. We know that on one occasion in the Sanhedrin he stood up for fair play in dealing with Jesus. We know that when Christ was crucified Nicodemus and Joseph of Arimathea took His body down from the cross, embalmed the body with spices and buried Jesus in Joseph's new tomb. We hope that this was a gesture of a redeemed heart, but we could wish that Nicodemus had made an open unashamed confession of his faith in Christ. This would have proved to us that he really had been born again.

Now think of the woman at the well. The Saviour dealt gently with her and showed her that she was a lost sinner. She gave her heart to Jesus out there by the well and in the joy of her salvation she left her waterpot and ran back into the city. "Come," she said to the people, "come, see a man who told me all that I ever did. Isn't this the Christ?" And we read that many of these Samaritans came out and believed on Christ because of her confession. There is no doubt that she was saved. She had Christ in her heart and she confessed Him before the world.

II. Sixty Seconds After Salvation We Have Been Given Eternal Life

When one is saved God gives him the same spiritual life that he will be having when he has been at home with God a million years from now. Twenty-five years ago a baby was born in a hospital. He weighed only a few pounds, he had to be pampered and coddled to enable him to live. But now he is six feet two inches tall and weighs 200 pounds. There is a vast difference in the baby and the man, yet the life he now has is the same life he had twenty-five years ago. And the spiritual life one receives the minute he is saved is the same spiritual life he will be living throughout eternity.

One morning I walked down the aisle of a church and confessed Christ as my personal Saviour. I was baptized that night. A few weeks later I was given a class of nine-year-old boys to teach. Then I learned to pray in public, to speak in the young people's group and to lead the weekly prayer meeting. Then even later God called me to preach and now for over forty years I have been proclaiming the Gospel of Christ. Yet the spiritual life I have now is the same spiritual life God gave me that day when He washed my sins away.

Our spiritual life grows here in the same manner that our physical life grows. We feed the physical body on physical food and engage in physical exercise and our physical bodies grow. If we feed our spiritual lives on spiritual food and engage in spiritual exercise, our spiritual lives will grow. Then one day when Jesus comes, in the twinkling of an eye, we will have perfect bodies, minds and spirits.

Yes, sixty seconds after salvation we have eternal lives, lives that never end. We live for Jesus now, we'll live with Jesus then. "He that believeth on the Son hath everlasting life" (John 3:36). We have that life sixty seconds after salvation.

III. Sixty Seconds After Salvation We Become the Children of God

John 1:12 says, "But as many as received him, to them gave he power to become the sons of God, even to them that believe on his name."

Today we hear many men proclaiming that all men are the

children of God. They want to be tolerant and broadminded. This sounds good, but it is not true to the Word of God. Jesus plainly taught that unregenerated men are the children of Satan. They become the children of God only when they come to Him through faith in His Son.

There are many advantages in having God as our Father. One is that we have direct access to Him through the Lord Jesus Christ. One day I was having lunch with a Catholic friend and I asked him why he prayed through the Virgin Mary. He said, "It is because she is closer to Jesus than anyone else and can therefore get His ear and attention." He said, "Suppose you wanted to have an interview with the president of the United States. You could not go to him direct, you would have to go through a senator or some other high official. It is the same way with coming to God. You must ask Mary to use her influence to get through to God." "But," I said, "suppose that I was the president's son, that I lived in the White House and ate at his table. Would I have to go through a senator to get to him? No, I would go straight to him, put my arms around him and make my wishes known." Well, I am a child of God, so I don't have to go through a human mediator to get to my heavenly Father. I go to Him in the name of Jesus and His heart is opened to me. I say, "Father, I am but a little child, but I am Your child. For Jesus' sake supply my need." And He will! Listen to Hebrews 4:14-16: "Seeing then that we have a great high priest, that is passed into the heavens, Jesus the Son of God, let us hold fast our profession. For we have not an high priest which cannot be touched with the feeling of our infirmities; but was in all points tempted like as we are, yet without sin. Let us therefore come boldly unto the throne of grace, that we may obtain mercy, and find grace to help in time of need."

Then there is I Timothy 2:5, "For there is one God, and one mediator between God and men, the man Christ Jesus."

Yes, sixty seconds after salvation we become the children

of God. That's better than being a child of a king, a president, a millionaire!

> I'm a child of the King,
> A child of the King;
> With Jesus my Saviour,
> I'm a child of the King.

IV. SIXTY SECONDS AFTER SALVATION OUR BODIES BECOME TEMPLES OF THE HOLY SPIRIT

"What? know ye not that your body is the temple of the Holy Ghost which is in you, which ye have of God, and ye are not your own?" (I Cor. 6:19).

Your body may be filled with sin, but when you become saved the blood of Jesus Christ cleanses you from sin and God the Holy Spirit comes to dwell in your heart and life.

"Jesus answered and said unto him, If a man love me, he will keep my words: and my Father will love him, and we will come unto him, and make our abode with him" (John 14:23). Some of us don't give Him much room in our hearts — they are cluttered up with other things — but if we are Christians the Holy Spirit lives in our hearts. He may be pushed off into a tiny corner, but He is still there. He is ready to comfort, to guide, to help when help is needed.

Dr. Scofield, the eminent Bible teacher, was once attending a Bible Conference in New York City. The chairman called on another minister to pray and his prayer went something like this: "Oh, thou great and terrible God, great is thy majesty. A great distance separates us from Thee. Poor lost sinners that we are, have mercy upon our souls." Dr. Scofield, when the prayer was ended, whispered to another preacher, "Why doesn't someone give that man a New Testament?" He was right. God is not far from a believer. Because of a believer's faith, because of his new birth, God is nearer to him than anyone on earth, for God the Holy Spirit dwells within him.

When our boys were young I would often go away for two

weeks to conduct a revival. The best part of the trip was always the return home. When I reached home the boys would run out to meet me. They did not say, "Oh, thou great and mighty evangelist, thou hast been gone for a prolonged season. We extend you a sincere welcome upon your return." No, they ran into my arms, hugged and kissed me and told me they were glad that I had come home. And it's like that with our heavenly Father. He is not a million miles away. He is very near and He wants us to feel the warmth of His loving arms.

The Christian's body is the temple in which the Holy Spirit dwells. A temple is a beautiful thing. It is set aside for God and must be kept clean. When Jesus found men defiling the temple He cast them out in anger. You and I are to remember that our bodies are temples of the Holy Spirit. And we must keep out of those temples anything that would defile or stain the dwelling place of the Holy Spirit. Yes, our bodies become temples of the Holy Spirit the minute we are saved and we must always keep those bodies as fit places in which the Spirit can dwell.

V. SIXTY SECONDS AFTER SALVATION WE BECOME SAINTS

What is a saint? Some people think that a saint is a perfect person, one who never sins. Yet no one ever measures up to that standard. Some people think that a saint is one who did good works while on earth and who is highly honored by ecclesiastical leaders after his death. But, according to the Bible, every born-again person is a saint. Anyone who comes out of sin, trusts in Christ and is born again instantly becomes a saint. The word saint means, "the holy one." We are not holy in our living but because of Christ we are holy in our position before God.

When you look through a blue glass everything looks blue. When you look through a red glass every thing has a reddish tinge. And when God looks at us through the blood of Christ He sees us in the white holiness of His own Son. We have the same position before Him that Christ has. The Bible tells us that when we come to Christ we are called "the righteous ones," "justified," "holy." This simply means that we are saints, all because of Christ.

One night Paul and Silas were in prison in Philippi. At midnight they sang praises to God and suddenly there was an earthquake which shook the jail. The doors were flung open and the prisoners were set free. The jailer, in his fear, was going to commit suicide. But Paul stopped him, talked to him about Jesus, and in a few minutes the man was saved. He might have had the marks of sin upon his body but immediately that body became the temple of the Holy Spirit. One minute the man was a child of Satan, the next moment he was a child of God. One moment he was on the way to hell, the next he possessed eternal life. All these changes came as soon as he saw himself as a lost sinner and surrendered in faith to the Saviour. In other words, he became a saint. He became a saint instantly when he came to Christ.

When we note the difference in our position and our condition we can understand the saint business better. Sometimes the believer's heart is swept by sin and he feels anything but a saint. His condition before God is not perfect, but his position is absolutely perfect. Nothing has changed. What, then, should be our concern? We ought to seek to live up to our high position as saints. If we have been born again, if we are the children of God, if we possess eternal life, if we are on the way to heaven to live forever with God, we ought to live like it.

Paul Rader became one of America's greatest preachers. But in his earlier life there was a lapse in his faith. He hardly believed the Bible, Christ or God. He was miserable. So he rented a hotel room, locked himself in and fell on his knees, praying that he might get back to God. He stayed in that room three days and nights. He got right with God and the Spirit filled his heart with joy and peace and power. He went out on the street in a happy mood. He looked up at an advertising sign which showed a kitten tangled up in some thread. "Little kitten," he said, "you are all tangled up, but, thank God, I'm free."

Do you remember when you were converted? A warm glow filled your heart. You were so happy that you had been saved, that you had passed from death unto life. Maybe as the years have gone by you have lost that feeling, that warm glow. But you can thank God that you haven't lost your position before God. You simply need to get right with God in your everyday life and practice. Come back to Him and live up to your high position as a saint.

A wealthy family of noble birth in England had a son who brought dishonor and shame to their good name because of his drunken scandals. The family finally told him they were going to cut off his quarterly allowance unless he left home. He then came to Canada where he wandered about, often spending his allowance before he received the next check. He then secured a job as an elevator operator at $15.00 per week. Later his father died and the young man became an earl. His young wife came over to Canada to take him home. He had a high position as a peer of England and a member of Parliament, but he was not living up to his high position. She took him home where he was elevated to his high position and where he lived up to it from that time on. Oh, friends, our position with God is much higher. God has given us a position higher than the angels in heaven. Yet we often forget this, we often sink down into sin. But may God help us to remember that we belong to Him and that we should live up to our high position.

A man went to a doctor for a physical examination. The doctor examined him thoroughly and said, "I can't find anything physically wrong with you." "But I'm suffering greatly," the man said, "there must be something wrong." Then the doctor said, "Have you done anything seriously wrong in your life recently?" The man became intensely angry and said, "I came for a check-up and not for a sermon. Send me my bill." And he stamped out of the office. Two weeks later he came back in a penitent mood. "Doctor," he said, "you had me right two weeks ago and I would not admit it. I cheated my brother out of a large sum of money. Now I can't sleep and I can't eat. Can you help me?"

The doctor replied, "Yes, I'll give you a prescription if you'll promise to take it." "I'll take it," said the man, "I need help." Then the doctor handed the man a sheet of paper and said, "First, write out a full confession to your brother."

With tears in his eyes, the man wrote out the confession. "Now," said the doctor, "write out a check and put it in the envelope with your confession." The man did this. "Now let's go out into the hall and put the letter in the mail slot." They walked out together and the letter and confession and check were soon on their way. Then the man said, "Doctor, down that chute goes the heaviest load a man ever carried. Thank God, I am rid of it now." "Yes," said the doctor, "but there is something else still to be done. You've made things right with your brother, now let's go back into my office and make things right with God." In the office the two men fell on their knees, the man confessed his sin to God and arose a new man, with peace in his heart.

Are you a child of God but not living up to your high position? Is there something between you and God, something between you and someone else? Then think of all the good things that are yours in Christ and show your gratitude by bringing your life up to what God would have it to be.

2

THE CHRISTIAN'S ACCOUNTING DAY

Matthew 25:14-30

When I was a boy I was given a job for the summer months as a "news butch" on a small railroad. The run was only twenty-one miles. We made two trips every day and three on Saturday and Sunday. At the end of the first week, when I checked in with my boss, I was forty cents short. This worried me greatly and I wondered where the shortage could have occurred. Then I found eight Coca-Cola bottles that had been broken and that accounted for the shortage. I was greatly relieved. You see, I wanted to check up squarely at the end of the week.

For many years now I have had the joy and privilege of serving Christ. He is coming back to check up some day and I want to check up squarely when I stand before His Judgment Seat. In my text we see a man going away for a long trip in a far country. He left his servants in charge of his business. To one he gave the equivalent of $1,200, to another $2,400 and to another $6,000. After a long time the man returned and checked up on these servants. Two of them had made a good record, but one had failed miserably to serve his master. The first two were commended. The other one was not only rebuked, he also was severely punished.

You can see the analogy here. Our Lord has gone away, but He is coming back some day. He has told us to "occupy" until He returns. We are to be busy for Him. Then, when

He comes back, there will be a great day of accounting. We will have to account to Him for the way we have used our talents and our lives. Some will be commended and rewarded, others will face Him in shame as they look back over their wasted lives.

The Christian must always remember that he owns nothing, not even himself. He belongs to Jesus. We were once the slaves of sin, but Jesus redeemed us with His own blood. Now we belong to Him. Paul says, "Ye are not your own, ye are bought with a price." And what a price it was. We have been "redeemed with the precious blood of Christ."

We are simply stewards; we are in this world to do business for Christ. And someday there'll be a great accounting day. When some Christians think of stewardship, they think only of money, but Bible stewardship involves much more. It covers not only money, but time, talents, service and all the life of a blood-bought child of the King.

I. WE ARE STEWARDS OF OUR PROPERTY

A man owns a piece of property. He turns it over to a real estate agency, they rent it to a tenant and collect the rent. But they don't keep all that they collect. The property is not theirs. They must make an accounting to the owner. In like manner, we don't own anything. We are simply to serve as stewards. Everything belongs to God and we are entrusted with it for only a short time. We don't own our salaries; it is God who gives us strength to earn these salaries. He asks that we bring Him one-tenth as a love offering, then the remaining nine-tenths is to be used in a way that will glorify Him. If you spend all your substance on yourself, what will you say to Christ on accounting day?

A Christian and a skeptic were discussing the merits of the Christian religion. When the Christian had extolled the virtues of Christianity, the skeptic said, "You might as well drop the subject. I don't believe these things and neither do you." "Yes, I do," said the Christian. "If you believed as you say," replied the non-Christian, "you would give something to it. I happen to know that in the past twenty years you haven't given as much to the church as you paid for your last cow." Yet, many Christians buy cars and homes and a good time, but give nothing to the Lord. A religion that costs nothing means nothing.

Someday you are going to face Christ. He will say, "I gave you power to make money. I endowed you with talent; I gave you strength and breath. Without Me you could have earned nothing. You know that My Book taught tithing. What did you do about it?" How can you face Him if you have been disoedient to Him. Your money is the least thing you can give God. In your giving you can perfectly do the will of God.

II. WE ARE STEWARDS OF OUR
OPPORTUNITIES TO HELP OTHERS

When I was a young preacher, I, like many others, had a difficult time financially. I had a wife and two children to support while I was in college and seminary. I had very little money to buy books, so a dear Christian woman helped me build up my library. She said, "I cannot preach, but I can buy books that will help you in your ministry." Another woman would send me a five-dollar bill once in a while and would say, "Use this to buy some gasoline for the car you use in the Lord's work." Both of these women saw an opportunity to help someone else and they used these opportunities.

A certain business man and his family lived in a rented house for many years. But they saved their money and the day finally came when they could say, "Now we can build a home for our own." Then they received a letter from a missionary in the Orient. The missionary told this couple that their small hospital had burned to the ground and that he had no place in which to house the many sick people who came to the mission station for help. The man looked at his wife and asked, "Which shall it be?" She replied, "The Lord gave us money for a house, but I believe He wants us to build it over there." So they sent their money to the missionary to be used in rebuilding the mission hospital and they continued to live in a rented house. They took advantage of an opportunity to help someone else and in due time God gave them a nicer home than the one they had dreamed of.

A dear old colored woman said, "Sis Ca'line come telling me about a poor family. She said she was so sad about them that she could shed a barrel of tears. Now that sho' is a lots of tears to shed for that poor family, but she ought to quit crying over them and cook them something to eat. Sis Ca'line takes out her sympathy in cryin' over the afflicted, but I ain't never heard her sob with her pocketbook." We know many people like her. It's cheaper to cry over people than it is to do something for them. But we are told that we are to "be doers of the word and not hearers only."

The sick are to be visited, the poor are to be clothed, the hungry are to be fed, souls are to be won. There are hundreds of opportunities all around us. The mark of a good Christian is that he is thoughtful of others.

> Lord, help me live from day to day
>   In such a self-forgetful way,
> That even when I kneel to pray,
>   My prayers will be for OTHERS.
>
> Help me in all the work I do,
>   To ever be sincere and true,
> And know that all I'd do for You,
>   Must needs be done for OTHERS.
>
> Let "self" be crucified and slain,
>   And buried deep; and all in vain
> May efforts be to rise again,
>   Unless to live for OTHERS.
>
> And when my work on earth is done,
>   And my new work in heav'n's begun,

May I forget the crown I've won,
While thinking still of OTHERS.

Others, Lord, yes, others,
Let this my motto be.
Help me to live for others,
That I may live like Thee.
— *Charles D. Meigs*

Someday we are going to face the Lord. He will say to us, "I spread opportunities all around you, opportunities for doing good. What did you do about them?" What can you answer Him in that day?

III. WE ARE STEWARDS OF OUR INFLUENCE

One man walks across a field and leaves a trail behind him. Another follows and another. Soon a clear path has been worn for men to walk in. It may be a straight path, it may be a crooked one. You are making a pathway for someone because of your influence. Will it be a straight path? Will others walk in the right way because of you?

Here are two men. One is supposed to be a Christian, the other one does not know the Saviour. This man offers the Christian a drink and he accepts. He does more than hurt himself; he loses his Christian influence right there. I heard some young men talking about drinking. Some of them thought drinking was perfectly all right. But one of them drew an imaginary circle around himself with his hands and said, "No drink will ever enter that circle." There is power and good influence in a life like that.

A certain warship went into action in the battle of Jutland. One of the men on board was a fine Christian named Stevens. All on board the ship knew that Stevens lived a clean life, prayed and read his Bible. As the ship moved into battle, nearly every man on board had to pass by Stevens' station. The word was passed along the line, "Touch Stevens, touch Stevens." As these men faced danger and possible death they wanted to touch a man who was in touch with God.

In the time of need the influence of Stevens counted for God. "A city that is set upon a hill cannot be hid." If the light of your life burns brightly for Christ, yours will be a beneficial influence.

And your influence doesn't die when you die. The Bible tells us that our works do follow us. Our influence will lift men or lower them after we have gone on to glory. It will be an influence for good or bad. Thomas Edison died but his influence lives on in the electrical world. Luther Burbank died but his influence lives on in the botanical world. Wilson and Roosevelt, Kennedy and Eisenhower are dead but their influence lives on in the political world. And if you and I live for Christ, our influence will live on in the spiritual realm.

A man came to Christ some time after his mother had died. He said, "I tried to be a skeptic, but my mother's Christian life was too much for me." She was living on after she had died.

Many children are going astray today because of the influence of their parents, parents who are living only for this world and leaving Christ out of their lives. Parents, I urge you to so live that your children can someday say, "I had the best father and mother that ever lived and I want to be like them." Someday you must account to God for your influence. How are you using it?

IV. We Are Stewards of Our Added Advantages

"To whom much is given, much shall be required." If you have a college education, if you can speak or sing well, if you have the ability to make money, more is required of you than those who do not have these advantages. If you have talents above others, you must answer to more than they.

Many years ago a Bombay physician said that he had discovered an effective cure for leprosy. He was urged to reveal his secret to the world. But he said, "My son is studying medicine and I'll pass the secret on down through him."

But one day the doctor was killed in an accident. The secret formula had not yet been given to his son, so it was lost to the world. The man had an added advantage, something that would have benefited mankind, but he robbed the world of it. If you have an added advantage, you have no right to withhold it.

One Christian has the power to sing, another to teach the Word, another to organize, another to bring men to Jesus. One day when we face Christ He will say, "I gave you some added advantages, what did you do with them?"

V. WE ARE STEWARDS OF THE GOSPEL OF CHRIST

We are living in a sinful world, God has given us a message for these times. Are you sharing the good news with others? Dr. Charles B. Howard was converted when he was a lad. The wife of a dying man asked him to talk to her husband about his relationship to Christ. He went to see the man and talked about everything else but Jesus. When he was leaving the house the man's wife said to him, "You left out the main thing. Why didn't you talk to him about his soul?" He replied, "I have just been converted and it's difficult for me to do that. But I promise you that I'll come back tomorrow and talk to him about his salvation." But the man died that night. Dr. Howard had let the opportunity slip by.

A preacher went to a London prison and witnessed to a man who had been sentenced to die. After he had talked to the man about Christ, the prisoner said, "Preacher, do you really believe all of that?" And the man said, "Yes, with all of my heart." Then the prisoner said, "If I believed it I would be willing to crawl on my knees all over England to tell the story." And if we realized the importance of salvation and man's need of it, surely we would want to tell the story.

Dr. Wilfred Grenfell had been a missionary in Labrador for forty years. Once he was given a banquet in his honor in an American city. A woman at the table said to him, "Is it true that you are a missionary?" He answered, "Isn't it true that you are?" Yes, it is every Christian's job to witness for Christ.

Dr. S. D. Gordon tells of a pastor who went to the home where a young woman had just died. He met his assistant who was in charge of the chapel which the young woman had attended and he asked the assistant if the young woman was a Christian. He answered, "No, I had a strong impulse to speak to her about the matter, but I never got around to it." He asked the young woman's Sunday school teacher the same question and received just about the same answer. Then he asked the young woman's mother about the matter and she said, "A voice within me told me to talk to her about salvation, but I didn't do it." All three of these Christians were stewards of the saving Gospel of Christ but they withheld their witness and the young woman went out to meet God unprepared.

Our city is full of lost people. Wouldn't it be a wonderful thing if every member of our church would win only one soul to Christ this year? Surely this is every Christian's job. You have no right to criticize the church or its leaders if you are not doing your best to win souls to Christ. Someday you are going to come face to face with God. He will say, "I saved you. You knew the way of salvation. Why didn't you tell that neighbor, that friend, about Me?" And what will your answer be?

VI. We Are Stewards of Our Talents

Our churches are full of talented people. Some of them are successful salesmen, some are great organizers, some have radiant personalities, some have the ability to make money. But all these talents are being used for self and the world. We could again turn the world upside down for Christ, as the early Christians did, if we would use all the talents God has given us in His service.

Someone gave a savage tribe a sundial. They loved it,

they thought it was beautiful, so they covered it over to protect it. Thus its usefulness was gone. God has given us many talents, but we bury them, we cover them up, we never use them for His glory. Someday God will call us to account for the way we have used or misused our talents.

When Stanley found David Livingstone in Africa, Livingstone said to him, "I would like to go back to England. My wife is dead, I would like to see the children and my friends there. The queen has invited me to come home and be 'knighted.' But I cannot go, I must finish my work here for God." He was using his talent to the very limit for God and humanity.

Al Staton was a famous football player at Georgia Tech. When he graduated as a mechanical engineer he was offered a job with a starting salary of $10,000 per year, which was a large salary in those days. But he turned down the job and went to Brazil as a missionary at a salary of $100 per month. He wanted to use all of his talents for God.

Someday we are going to face Christ at the Judgment Seat. He will say, "I gave you certain talents down there in the world. How did you use them, for the world or for me?" What will your answer be?

VII. We Are Stewards of Our Whole Lives

You have one little life. What are you doing with it? In that day Jesus will say, "My church was down there. Why were you not faithful to it? I had a work for you to do down there. Why didn't you do it?" Your excuses for not serving God may satisfy you now, but they won't stand up at the Judgment. May God help the poor lean Christian who is doing nothing for God and who must someday give an account to Him.

A tourist in Southern California was admiring some beautiful flowers in front of a lovely home. A lady came out of the house and was very cordial to the tourist. She took her scissors, snipped off several flowers and gave them to the

stranger. The tourist thanked her and started back toward
her car. As she did every petal fell off the flowers the lady
had given her. That's the way it is with many of us. We
waste our lives for the world, then present God only the
faded petals. Billy Sunday said that "some men burn their
candles out for Satan, then blow the smoke in God's face
at the end of the way."

The old adage says, "Don't burn the candle at both ends."
But Henry van Dyke said, "I'll rather burn it at both ends
and in the middle, too, than to put it in a dark closet for
the mice to eat." We are saved to serve. We are to let our
light shine for God. Don't wait until life is coming to an
end before you begin to use that life for God.

When you face God and He says, "I gave you life and all
of its opportunities, what did you do with it?" what can you
say to Him?

Let us look in on a scene at the Judgment Seat. As Paul
stands before the Saviour, Jesus says to him, "Paul, what did
you do with the life, the intellect, the talents I gave you?"
And Paul will say, "I gave you my best. For thirty years I
preached and served and suffered for you in Asia and in
Europe. I counted all things but loss that I might know and
follow you." And Jesus will say, "Well done, enter into the
joys of your Lord."

Then a poor working girl will come before the Lord and
He will say, "You didn't have many opportunities, but what
did you do with the opportunities you did have?" And she
will reply, "Lord Jesus, there was a girl who worked right
next to me and I told her about You and she was saved.
I didn't do much for You." But then Jesus will say, "Well
done, enter into the joys of your Lord. Stand over there by
Paul."

Then Billy Graham will stand before the great Judge and
Jesus will say, "I gave you marvelous preaching talent. I
gave you the radio and television and great crowds. What
did you do with these advantages?" And Billy Graham can
say, "Lord, I used every one of them for Your glory. I told

people about You all over the world and pled with men to give their hearts and lives to You." Then the Master will say, "Well done, good preacher, enter into the joys of your Lord:"

Then a poor, uneducated man will stand before the Saviour. "You did not have many opportunities," says the Lord. "You were never far from the place where you were born. But what did you do with these limited opportunities?" And the man will say, "My neighbor was lost. I told him about You as well as I could and he accepted You as his Saviour." And Jesus will say, "Well done, my child, enter into the joys of your Lord. Take your place with Paul and Billy Graham and all of the saints." Yes, the great and the small will be rewarded if they have been faithful stewards.

In Louisiana a schoolteacher taught in a rural school. All the children were very poor, but her beautiful Christian life won their love. Instead of the schoolroom having a door there was nothing but an open space and in February the cold wind from the marshes swept into the room, chilling the poorly-clad children. So this godly teacher stood in the doorway and shielded the children from the cold. But her love cost her her life. She contacted pneumonia and died in a few days.

"Greater love hath no man than this, that a man lay down his life for his friends" (John 15:13). But shall I tell you of a greater love than that of the godly schoolteacher? Then I must tell you of the Lord Jesus, who turned His back to the smiters for you and me, who died on the cross for you and me, who bled His life away for you and me. His love for us cost Him His life. You are going to face Him some- day. What will you say to Him when He says,

> I gave My life for thee,
> My precious blood I shed,
> That thou might'st ransomed be,
> And quickened from the dead;
> I gave, I gave My life for thee —
> What hast thou giv'n for Me?

3

WHO CARES FOR YOUR SOUL?

Psalm 142:4

Of all the Old Testament characters, I believe David is my favorite. I like him because he is so human, so much like the rest of us. He was never a plaster saint. He was tremendously human, always falling down, yet always getting up and reaching out toward the God he loved and served.

Some days he was a great saint, some days a great sinner. Some days he was so close to God that he could write the 23rd Psalm. One day he was so forgetful of God that he broke at least four of the Ten Commandments. One day he was in such deep despair that he cried out, "No man cared for my soul." On another day he was on the mountain top, saying, "The Lord is my refuge and my portion."

Yes, David was like the rest of us and we like him for it. We, too, have our ups and downs, our mountain tops and our valleys, our moments of despair and our moments of glory. But if we belong to God, through faith, as David did, we will always be reaching out toward God and a better life. We can say with the old spiritual:

> I'm sometimes up and sometimes down,
> But praise the Lord, I'm heavenward bound.

Now in our text we see that David was in the ditch of despair. He said that he looked all around him and found that no man cared for his soul. Surely he had a bad case of the blues. I have known people who felt the same way. I have heard them say, "Nobody cares for me; nobody cares whether I go to hell or not." In this message I will try to show you how badly mistaken you are.

I. GOD CARES FOR YOUR SOUL

Go back to the Garden of Eden and you see our first parents falling into sin. And in their fall they caused the virus of sin to enter every one who is born into the world. Now God is a God of justice. When His law is broken His justice says that punishment must follow. What, then, is the punishment for God's broken law? It is the eternal prison house called hell.

So God looked down on lost men and saw them going to hell. This moved His great compassionate heart and made Him say, "I must do something about this. I must give sinful man a way of escape." Then He looked for someone to bear all the sins of mankind. That one must himself be without sin. Is there one in heaven who meets these requirements? Can Abraham or Moses or Elijah stand the test? No, for everyone of them had sinned in some way.

Then God's glance lighted on His only begotten Son. He was the only One who could stand the test, the only One without sin. So God said, "Son, will You go to earth and redeem mankind? Will You go and die in order to save lost humanity?" And Jesus answered, "Yes, Father, I'll go. Greater love hath no man than this, that a man lay down his life for his friends." And when this decision was made the angels in heaven began loudly to voice their protests. "No," they cry. "No, God's only begotten Son must not go. He is the Prince of glory; He is the bright and morning star; He is the fairest among ten thousand, the One altogether lovely. Why should the sinless Son of God die for sinful men?"

But "God so loved the world." So Jesus came to earth and lived among men. He was "a man of sorrows and acquainted with grief." He was mistreated on every side and finally cruel men took Him out and nailed Him to a cross. And God from heaven looked down upon it all. As the sufferings of Jesus on earth broke the heart of God in heaven, what was God saying to us? He was saying, "I do care for your soul. Look to Calvary. I gave my only Son for you."

We remember during World War II how a telegram would come to a family, saying, "The War Department regrets to inform you that your son has been killed in action." These telegrams broke the hearts of many fathers and mothers back in America, far from the firing line. But they didn't see how their sons died. They didn't see how the machine-gun bullets cut them down. They didn't see the blood streaming from broken bodies. They didn't hear the agonizing cries. They only knew that a son was dead.

But how different it was with God. He saw His Son die, He saw it all. He saw the wounds, the blood. He heard the agonizing cry, "My God, my God, why hast thou forgotten me?" Yes, the heavenly Father saw it all and it broke His heart. And all the time He was saying, "I love you; I do care for your soul. Look what I gave to save you from hell." Don't ever say no one cares for your soul. God cares.

II. Christ Cares for Your Soul

He had the highest place in heaven; He was the central figure in glory. The angels and the archangels ran to do His bidding. Then when He heard the cry of lost men on earth, He turned away from all the glory of heaven and sped down to earth to become the humblest Man in the world and to die for our sakes.

He was born of a virgin. The Holy Spirit reduced Christ in size to one little cell in order that He might come down and be born of a woman. Oh, what condescension! And all the time Jesus was just saying, "I care for your soul."

When Jesus was born Mary laid Him in a manger. Look at that tiny Babe. Is that the One who created the heavens and the earth? Is that the One who made man? Is that the One who rules the destinies of nations? Yes, it is; that's

God's Son. But now He is reduced to a tiny baby. He must go through all the temptations and troubles that beset mankind for our sakes. He is just saying, "I care for your soul."

During His public ministry He was called every evil name under the sun. He was humiliated in every way known to man. Then one dark night they arrested Him and took Him to Pilate's court. They pressed the crown of thorns upon His brow; they spat in His face and slapped Him. They took the cat-o-nine tails and beat Him until blood ran down His back. And when the morning came they laid a heavy cross on His back and led Him down the Via Dolorosa. And He was saying, "See, all of this is for you. I do care for your soul."

When they reached the hill of Golgotha they threw His body down on that cross; they drove great spikes through His hands and feet; they lifted that cross high above the earth with its divine burden on it. There for six long hours in agonizing pain He bled His life away for you and me. And as He died, crying out, "It is finished," He was simply saying, "I do care for your soul. All this is for you. I do this to save you from hell."

> See, from His head, His hands, His feet,
> Sorrow and love flow mingled down;
> Did e'er such love and sorrow meet,
> Or thorns compose so rich a crown?

Yes, Jesus cares for your soul.

III. THE HOLY SPIRIT CARES FOR YOUR SOUL

Who is the Holy Spirit? He is a Person, the third Person of the Godhead. Few Christians have gone deeply enough in their spiritual lives to know much about Him. They know about God the Father and God the Son, but little or nothing about God the Holy Spirit. Yet all the way through the Bible He is co-equal with the Father and the Son. To put it simply, God the Holy Spirit is the God who works and operates in human hearts today. Before Jesus returned to heaven He said, "I am going to send the Holy Spirit to take My place on earth. The first thing He will do will be to convict men of sin and righteousness and judgment to come."

And this is the first work He is doing now in human hearts. He comes to us and says, "You are not right with God. You have sinned. And someday you must face judgment and give account for the deeds done in the flesh." After having pointed out our sins He then points to the only One who can save us from our sins. He says, "You need a Saviour. Look, here He is, dying for you on the cross. Turn from your sin and put all your faith in Him and you'll be saved."

In my first pastorate I had been talking to a man about taking Christ as his Saviour. He came to church a number of times but made no move toward accepting the Saviour. One night I saw him sitting there in the church with another man. During the invitation period I felt led to go down and speak to him. I had to lean over the other man to talk to him. He refused again, saying, "Some other time." But the other man, to whom I said nothing, said to me, "I'll take Christ as my Saviour." And he came forward and made his public profession of faith. The Holy Spirit had spoken to both men, one responded and the other didn't. And a man's eternal destiny is determined by his response to the Holy Spirit.

I was preaching in a revival in Gastonia, North Carolina. A fine young man came each night and sat by his wife. But he was not a Christian. On the last night of the meeting I saw him there and began to pray definitely that the Holy Spirit would get hold of him that night and bring him to the Saviour. The church was filled with people, but I pointed my message to this young man, although he didn't know it. When the invitation was given he was the first one to come forward. The Holy Spirit had done His work.

I was holding the first meeting of my life in a little church in Atlanta. On the last day of the meeting I called my unsaved brother, seven years older than myself, and invited him to come to church. He said, "I'm not in the habit of going to church." "But," I said, "Papa is coming up from our old home and will be at church. I thought maybe you'd like to see him." And my brother said, "Well, I'll come out to see him." He came and had to listen to the sermon and the Holy Spirit began to work in his heart. I didn't have a car then, so that afternoon he surprised me by phoning me and saying, "I'll come by and take you to church tonight." I began to pray for the Holy Spirit to convict him and point him to the Saviour. The little church was so crowded that night that my brother had to sit on the floor. I preached and gave the invitation. My brother was the first one to come forward, weeping. He said, "I should have done this long ago." The Holy Spirit had done His work.

Any preacher who has served God over the years could tell you of hundreds of such examples. When the Holy Spirit comes to convict men and point them to Christ, He is simply saying, "I care for your soul. I do this to save you from hell."

IV. THE CHURCH CARES FOR YOUR SOUL

Why do we build churches all over the land? Why do we employ pastors and church staffs? Why do we have the various organizations in the church? Why do we give our tithes and offerings? For one reason only — because we want you to be saved.

Some people say that we have churches for one purpose only, to provide a place of worship for God. I do agree that people ought to attend church and worship the Lord. But that is not the only purpose of the church. We are not to shut ourselves up in an ivory tower and just let the rest of the world go by. As we worship God we must remember that there are those who do not know the Saviour and we must seek to win them to Christ.

A church is not simply a mass of bricks and stone — it is people. And we do care for souls. Our highest joy comes when we see someone coming to Christ for salvation. Our highest duty is to let men know that we care for their souls. A young man languished in the death cell of a prison. A godly woman visited him and talked to him about salvation. He said to her, "In all my life no one ever spoke to me about my soul until I was brought to this terrible place of death. If someone had shown an interest in my soul, perhaps I never would have been here." A certain man made three trips around the world. He talked to thousands of people in every walk of life. Only two of them ever said anything to him about his soul. Another man was a railroad conductor for fifteen years. He was asked all kinds of questions about schedules, connections, the weather, his family and a thousand other things. Finally after fifteen years a man asked him if he were a Christian.

Every church ought to care for souls. In the last book of the Bible we read, "The Spirit and the Bride say, come." The bride referred to here is the church of the Lord Jesus Christ. Those of us in the church do care for your soul. We sometimes neglect to manifest our interest, but all we do in our church say to you, "We care for your soul; we want to see you saved."

V. The People in Heaven Care for Your Soul

Jesus tells us that there is more rejoicing in heaven over one sinner who is saved than over ninety-nine who need no repentance. And why do these hosts of heaven rejoice? Because they know how wonderful heaven is and they want you to come up and enjoy it.

Some people think that the saints in heaven know everything that goes on down here upon the earth. They quote the Scripture that says we "are encompassed about with so great a cloud of witnesses." We are not sure that our loved ones in heaven can see all that goes on down here. Some of it might cause sorrow even in heaven. But I do believe it is true when souls are saved, they know it and rejoice over it.

I can imagine some mother dying and leaving a little boy

down here on earth. Then one day after the boy grows up he goes to church and is saved. The angel that has been watching over that boy flies to his mother's mansion and says, "Your boy has been saved. Now he is a child of God." Then I can hear that mother shouting all over God's heaven and saying to everyone up there, "Rejoice with me, my boy has been saved and some day he'll be up there with Jesus and me."

Nobody can fully describe heaven. No tongue can tell of all of its glories, and no mind can even imagine how wonderful it will be. But our friends and loved ones up there know. They know how many good things God has laid up for those who love Him. They know how sweet it is to be with Jesus. And they want us to share in it all. So I say that those up in heaven care for your soul.

VI. THE PEOPLE IN HELL CARE FOR YOUR SOUL

This is a solemn thought but it's in the Bible. Jesus said that a rich man died and went to hell. That man cried out and said that he was tormented in the flames of that awful place. Then he looked up and saw Lazarus the beggar and Abraham in heaven. He said to Father Abraham, "I want to ask you one little favor. Send Lazarus down and let him dip the tip of his finger in water and put it on my burning lips." And Abraham replied, "I can't do that. There is a great gulf fixed between you and us. We can't come down there and you can't come up here." Then the poor rich man said, "Well, if you can't do that, please send Lazarus to warn my brothers to get right with God, so that they won't come to this place of torment."

So you can see that those in hell know how awful the place is. They care for your soul; they don't want you to live without Christ and finally come down to hell.

Therefore, don't ever say that no one cares for your soul. God cares, Christ cares, the Holy Spirit cares, the church cares, those in heaven care, and those in hell care.

But do you care? Is it well with your soul? Are you prepared to meet God? If not, you'll never find a better time than right now. "Today, if you hear his voice, harden not your heart."

In 1948 I conducted a revival in the First Baptist Church of Ada, Oklahoma. On Sunday morning a young blind man sang a beautiful solo, "I'm praying for you." The congregation was moved to tears as he sang. Later the pastor told me the story behind the young man's blindness. When he was ten years of age his father, who was not a Christian, took him hunting on Sunday, saying that there was "no harm in going hunting on the Lord's Day." At one place his father told the boy to wait for him while he circled the field. Seeing what he thought was a squirrel's tail the father fired his shotgun. He then heard an agonizing cry and ran to his boy. What he thought was a squirrel's tail was the boy's hair waving in the wind and the father had accidently shot his own son. In great distress he gathered the boy in his arms and rushed him to the nearest hospital. The boy's life was saved but he lost his eyesight. The weeping father said, "This would not have happened if I hadn't been hunting on Sunday."

In the next revival in that church the boy was saved. Soon he had won his father and mother to Christ. Later the pastor checked the records and found that he had baptized forty-one converts, all of whom were won to Christ because of the influence of that boy. Later as a young man he said, "If it took my blindness to bring these to Christ, I am glad to go blind through life."

That boy gave his eyes but there was one who gave more than that to save you and me. Jesus gave His all on Calvary that we might have eternal life. Won't you take Him as your Saviour? Then you can truly say, "No one ever cared for me like Jesus."

4

THE HOLY SPIRIT IN THE LIFE OF A BELIEVER

John 14:16-18

I remember that when I was a boy, years before I was converted, I would often hear a preacher speak of the Holy Spirit. I had no idea what he was talking about. I am afraid that there are many church members like that today.

We know what is meant when the preacher speaks of God the Father. He created the world, fixes the destinies of men and nations, and is the Father of Jesus Christ. We know what is meant when we hear about God the Son. We know that He was born in Bethlehem, that He lived in Nazareth, that He preached and taught and healed for over three years. We know that He died on the cross, that He rose from the grave, that He ascended up on high and that He is coming again.

But what is meant by God the Holy Spirit? He is the third Person of the Trinity, co-equal with the Father and the Son. He is the God who operates in the human heart. Before Jesus went back to heaven He said to His disciples, "I am not going to leave you alone. I am going to send you Someone who will take My place, even God the Holy Spirit. He will dwell forever in your heart. He will comfort you, will lead you in the paths of righteousness, and will guide you all the way to glory."

And on the day of Pentecost He came. It was a day of power and glory. He filled the disciples with power. He caused them to speak in other languages, and three thousand people were saved in a day. Now he lives in the heart of every born-again believer. The simplest way I know to describe Him is to say that He is God in the heart of the Christian.

His first work is that of conviction for sin. I was a sinner, lost and on the way to hell, but I didn't know it. Then I attended an evangelistic service where the ways of life and death were made plain. Something happened to me. I saw myself as a lost sinner. I was convicted for my sin. I realized my lost condition, and I wept bitter tears. Next He pointed me to the Saviour. I was like a man in a deep, dark hole with no way of escape. Then I saw a light and a ladder leading out of that hole. I started to climb out and then I felt a pair of strong arms around me. Jesus was lifting me out of that hole. He saved me, washed my sins away, gave me peace and great joy. But it was the Holy Spirit who convicted me and pointed me to that Saviour. He performed the first work of grace in my heart and now, even as Jesus promised, He dwells within my heart.

Now starting from this point, let us see what He does in the life of a believer. I will use several words to describe His work. They are regeneration, sanctification, confirmation, consolation, supplication, illumination and translation.

I. Regeneration

Nicodemus came to Jesus by night. He was a hungry-hearted man, seeking hope and satisfaction for this life and the life to come. Jesus said to him, "You must be born again." And He told him that the Holy Spirit was the agent in regeneration. Every man comes into the world through a physical birth, but that is not enough. He needs a spiritual birth. How does he get it? It comes through the work of the Holy Spirit when that man comes to Jesus the Saviour. A new nature is given to him, but he still retains the old carnal nature. These two natures are in constant warfare, but the believer has the Holy Spirit to help him when temptations arise.

The greatest need of every man is to be born again, to be re-born of the Spirit. A cynical lost man said to a preacher, "You spoke of the weight of sin. I don't feel any weight. How much is it, fifty pounds, a hundred pounds?" And the preacher said "Can a dead body feel any weight placed upon it?" "No," said the man, "a dead man couldn't feel it if you placed a thousand pounds on him." "Well," said the preacher, "that's the way it is with you. You are dead in your sin and therefore can't feel the weight of it." Now it is the work of the Holy Spirit which makes you feel that weight. The only way that a dead man can find life is through the regenerating power of the Holy Spirit.

We see that a man is born again when he repents of his sin and trusts Christ as his Saviour. But all of this is brought about by the Holy Spirit. It is not of ourselves. Our conviction, our repentance, our faith are produced by the Holy Spirit. Now this is not an automatic thing. We don't just stand aside and say, "I am going to do nothing. I am simply going to let the Holy Spirit save me if He wants to do it." No, we must permit Him to work; we must surrender our wills to His. Then He can work in us and bring about salvation.

One who is born can't be unborn. I was born of my father and mother and I'll always be their child, regardless of my actions. And since I am born of the Spirit I'll always be God's Child. I may go astray. I may displease Him, but I am His because I have been born of the Spirit. He has power to save and power to keep. Regeneration is a complete process. The Holy Spirit begins and completes His work in us. Christ said that if we came to Him, He would not cast us out. He said that no man would be able to pluck us out of the Father's hand. And the Holy Spirit is the One who keeps us safe from grace to glory.

Listen to Romans 8:1, "There is therefore now no condemnation to them which are in Christ Jesus, who walk not after the flesh, but after the Spirit."

II. SANCTIFICATION

Some Christians are afraid of this word because it has been used in the wrong sense in times past. We have heard people say that they are sanctified and they meant that they were absolutely perfect. They are wrong. Christians are right in their position toward God, but never in practice. Sanctification is a good word, a Bible word.

The primary meaning of sanctification has the idea of being set apart for God's use. When the temple was built it was sanctified, that is, it was set aside for a purpose, for the worship of God. When we build a new church we have a right to say that it is sanctified, it is set apart for worship, for the preaching of the Gospel, for the winning of the lost and the blessing of the saved, for the glory of God.

Suppose we used our church auditorium for a dance or a rodeo or a rummage sale. That would be blasphemy. It has been set apart for a nobler and higher purpose. Well, when a person comes to Christ he is set apart from the world for a purpose. He is to serve God and glorify Him forever. If he gives his life to the low things of sin and the world, he dishonors God. You can see then that in this sense every Christian is sanctified, or set apart for God's purposes.

"What? know ye not that your body is the temple of the Holy Ghost which is in you, which ye have of God, and ye are not your own?" (I Cor. 6:19). Since the body is the temple of God the Holy Spirit, He ought to have a clean place in which to dwell. We ought to keep our bodies clean. Nothing should touch them that would defile His temple.

Let me illustrate this thought of being set apart for a purpose. When World War II began our factories were building automobiles and tires and tractors and many other things. Then they were converted to another purpose. They began to build tanks, planes and guns. They had been set aside for a new purpose. In like manner we once were serving Satan. He ruled our hearts and lives. Then we were converted. Now we have been set apart for a new purpose. Old things must be thrown out and we must serve Christ.

"Therefore if any man be in Christ, he is a new creature: old things are passed away; behold, all things are become new" (II Cor. 5:17). Yes, life is altogether different after a person has been genuinely converted. When he comes to Christ he says, "I am turning my life over to my Lord. I want Him to put His hand on me. I want the world to know that I have been set aside for His service and His glory."

Another phase of sanctification is growth in grace. This is also the work of the Holy Spirit. When we let Him fill our hearts, it causes us to grow in grace and we become stronger Christians as the days go by. We read the Bible, we pray, we give, we go to church, we serve. The Holy Spirit uses all of these things to nurture our spiritual growth.

Here is a couple looking at their first baby. Physically the child is normal in every way, but as the days pass they learn that the child's mind is a blank. He grows strong and tall but he is an imbecile. He never speaks, and never recognizes anyone. His condition grieves his parents. Now here is one who has just been saved. He has been born of the Spirit and has become a child of God. But the years go by and there is no growth. He bears no fruit, and gives God no service. Surely this must grieve the heart of God for He wants His children to grow spiritually.

We are told that a wasp is larger at birth than at any other time. Some Christians are like that. They are more spiritual and more active for God when they are born again than at any future time. They get out of communion with God. They leave His service, and forget His church.

The Holy Spirit sanctifies and sets Christians aside for God's service. What a pity that so many of them get out of God's corral and into the devil's pasture. Just stay close to Him and you will grow in grace. You will be a joy to God and a blessing to others and yourself.

III. Confirmation

Our salvation is confirmed in heaven. "Grieve not the Holy Spirit of God, whereby ye are sealed unto the day of redemption (Eph. 4:30). When the president of the United States signs a bill that has been passed by Congress, the Secretary of State places the official seal upon the document and then the whole authority of the United States is behind it. When a person comes to Christ, God saves that soul, and the Holy Spirit then sets His seal on that soul. And no power in heaven or earth can break the seal.

"And I give unto them eternal life; and they shall never perish, neither shall any man pluck them out of my hand. My Father, which gave them me, is greater than all; and no man is able to pluck them out of my Father's hand" (John 10:28, 29). Billions of dollars' worth of gold is buried in Fort Knox. This treasure is encased in buildings of steel and iron and guarded by many soldiers. We say this gold is safe, but it isn't one-half as safe as a soul which has trusted Jesus. That soul, sealed by the Spirit, is safe for all the countless ages of eternity.

Not only does the Holy Spirit confirm our salvation in heaven, but He also confirms it in our hearts. "The Spirit itself beareth witness with our spirit, that we are the children of God" (Rom. 8:16).

How can one know that he is saved? There are many tests but here we are told that the Spirit within us witnesses with His Spirit that we are God's children. This is something we can't explain to others. It must be experienced in one's own heart. But a voice deep within says, "You are mine; I bought you on the cross. When you trusted Me you passed from death to life and you'll never come into condemnation."

"For as many as are led by the Spirit of God, they are the sons of God. For ye have not received the spirit of bondage again to fear; but ye have received the Spirit of adoption, whereby we cry, Abba, Father" (Rom. 8:14, 15).

When one becomes a Christian he is no longer under

bondage; he does not live in fear. He has been adopted into a great family. He calls God, "Father." So we see how the Holy Spirit confirms our salvation.

IV. CONSOLATION

"And I will pray the Father, and he shall give you another Comforter, that he may abide with you forever" (John 14:16). "As one whom his mother comforteth, so will I comfort you" (Isa. 66:13).

That's the work of the Holy Spirit, to comfort the believer in the time of trouble, like a mother comforts her child. My mother died just before I reached my fourth birthday. Many little hurts came to me as a child and I had no one to comfort me. I was told that my mother had gone to heaven, so often in my loneliness I wished that I could go up to heaven and have her comfort me. Now that's what the Holy Spirit does. He comes into our hearts to abide forever, then when sorrow comes He puts His arms around us and says, "Be not afraid, I am with you. I will never leave you nor forsake you. I'll cause all things to work together for your good."

One morning I received the news that the little daughter of one of my deacons had died during the night. I went over to the home, put my arms around his shoulders and sought to comfort him. Then, looking at me through his tears, he said, "Preacher, it's all right, it's all right." How could he say that when his heart was breaking? He could say it because of the comforting power of the Holy Spirit.

Four men were eating dinner on a railroad dining car one night. The waiter seemed to be very nervous. The men had to ask him several times for some water and the salad never came. When he served the dessert he said, "I want to apologize for my service this evening." One of the men assured him that it was all right. They realized he was new on the job. "No, sir," he said. "I have served for years. But this afternoon, just before I left Mississippi, I received a call telling me that my little girl had been killed on the streets of New York. We are short of men so I felt it my duty to go on, but I am terribly nervous." One of the four men was a minister. He took his New Testament out of his pocket and the waiter said, "I know that book. The only thing that keeps me going tonight is the truth of Christ in that book." You see, the Holy Spirit is a comforter. He takes the things of Christ and brings them to our minds, comforting us in time of sorrow.

V. SUPPLICATION

"Likewise the Spirit also helpeth our infirmities: for we know not what we should pray for as we ought: but the Spirit itself maketh intercession for us with groanings which cannot be uttered. And he that searcheth the hearts knoweth what is the mind of the Spirit, because he maketh intercession for the saints according to the will of God" (Rom. 8:26, 27).

We can pray and we thank God for the privilege, but we can never offer a perfect prayer. However, the Holy Spirit knows what is best for us and prays for us according to the will of God. These prayers are not perfunctory; they are "groanings." Did you ever pray that way? Did you ever weep your way to God? Well, that is how the Holy Spirit really prays for us.

We are reminded that we can pray for the power of the Holy Spirit. Look at the disciples. They had everything to fit them for service, but they were not ready. They had Calvary, the resurrection, the commission, and they had the promise. But they were not ready to witness until the Holy Spirit came.

We pray for the Spirit to fill us and He is ready to do just that. But He can't do it if our lives are filled with sin and self. There are many people with wonderful talents, but they are not being used of God. It is because all they do is of self and not for the glory of God. All of us need to empty our hearts of sin and self and pray for the Holy Spirit to take over.

VI. Illumination

The Holy Spirit illumines the pages of the Bible for us. That's the reason that a sinful man cannot understand the Bible. He doesn't have the Holy Spirit to guide his understanding.

"But God hath revealed them unto us by his Spirit: for the Spirit searcheth all things, yea, the deep things of God. Now we have received, not the spirit of the world, but the spirit which is of God; that we might know the things that are freely given to us of God" (I Cor. 2:10, 12).

I go up to see a great castle. I have heard of its beauties within, but I have never seen these beauties. I stand before the door and I see nothing of the beauty. I have no key and I cannot enter. Then the owner of the castle comes. He has a key. He opens the door, leads me in and takes me from room to room. He shows me the beauties of the castle and explains its mysteries. Now the Bible is full of beauty and mystery. I stand before it but I have no key to unlock its door. Then the Holy Spirit comes. He leads me through its pages; He shows me its beauties and explains its mysteries.

The Holy Spirit not only illumines the pages of the Bible, but He also lights up the pathway of the believer. You and I come often to the crossroads. Which way shall we go? Which way is best? If we trust our own wisdom we will often go the wrong way. Jesus said the Holy Spirit would teach us. Surely He knows the way better than we do. We need to follow His guidance.

If any of you lack wisdom, let him ask of God, that giveth to all men liberally, and upbraideth not; and it shall be given him" (James 1:5). If you are selecting a life career, ask for the guidance of the Holy Spirit. If you plan to marry, if you want to change jobs or buy a house, ask for this guidance. "In all thy ways acknowledge him, and he shall direct thy paths" (Prov. 3:6).

VII. TRANSLATION

"But if the Spirit of him that raised up Jesus from the dead dwell in you, he that raised Christ from the dead shall also quicken your mortal bodies by his Spirit that dwelleth in you" (Rom. 8:11).

There are two pathways that lead a believer from earth to heaven. First, it may be the pathway of death. The man without Christ has a right to fear death for he doesn't know what is coming. He knows that he is going out to meet God and he knows that he is not ready. But the Christian need not fear death. It simply becomes a servant to transport him from a sinful earth to heaven.

When a Christian dies the Holy Spirit takes his soul up to be with Christ. This is according to the teachings of the New Testament. The body is then buried, but in the great resurrection morning the Holy Spirit will raise the body. Christ will bring back the soul, and body and soul will be joined, to be forever with the Lord.

But suppose the Lord comes in the air while we are living. Then the Holy Spirit will catch up every Christian in the world, change them into the likeness of Christ and take them to heaven. So, whether we go up to heaven through death or through the rapture it will be the Spirit who translates us.

Dr. E. W. Perry, great negro preacher of Oklahoma City, told this story of the resurrection at one of our conventions. He said that a great serpent swam through the water and swallowed many small fish alive. Soon he swallowed a larger fish with sharp fins. Down in the serpent's stomach this large fish said, "I don't like darkness. I am going to get out of here." So he began to use his sharp fins on the serpent and soon he had cut his way out and was free. This killed the serpent, and as the large fish swam out, all the other fish followed him.

Well, that serpent was the monster, death. Down over the ages he has been swallowing God's people. Then one day he swallowed Jesus. And Jesus, in the grave, said, "I don't

like it in here in the darkness, so I am going to get out."
By the power of the Holy Spirit He conquered death and
came out to live forever. Now all who believe in Him, though
they are dead, shall follow Him into eternal life. "Because
he lives, we shall live also."

Yes, the Holy Spirit is the Christian's best friend in this
world. We are regenerated by His power, sealed unto the
day of redemption, sanctified and our salvation confirmed.
Our hearts are consoled and the pathway of life is lighted
up. He is praying for us, and at last by His power we are
translated and taken up to be with Jesus and like Him forever. What a Friend He is indeed!

A man wanted to see the sunrise from a certain mountain
top. He drove up the mountain road in his car. But the car
was old. It "chugged" along for a while, but finally gave up.
So the man got out and walked the rest of the distance to
see the glorious sunrise. The Holy Spirit is walking along
with us toward the sunrise of eternal glory. After a while
these old bodies will give out and we will lay them aside.
Then the Holy Spirit will take us by the hand and lead us
into the presence of the King. Soon all the wonders of heaven
will burst upon our sight.

Won't you open up your heart to Jesus? Then the Holy
Spirit will come in and walk with you until He takes you
home.

5

GOD'S LAST INVITATION

Revelation 22:17

Sometime ago I went down to the shipyard where many government ships were brought in for repair. A big sign on the main building said to me, "Keep Out." I have often seen signs on office doors, saying, "Private, no admission." Sometimes I have seen a sign saying, "Keep off the grass." The hunter who goes out in the country in search of game sees the sign, "Land posted, keep off." Now this is man's way. But God's way is different. He opens up every door and says to the sinner, "Come in, come in and be saved. Come in and enjoy all I have for you in two worlds."

God's great purpose in redemption is very clear. Man is lost in sin. God gave His Son to redeem them, and now He invites everyone to come to Him through Christ and be saved. This note runs all the way through the Bible like a river running through a valley. In Isaiah we read, "Ho, every one that thirsteth, come to the waters, and he that hath no money; come ye, buy, and eat; yea, come, buy wine and milk without money and without price" (Isa. 55:1). Again we hear these words in Isaiah 1:18, "Come now, and let us reason together, saith the Lord: though your sins be as scarlet, they shall be as white as snow; though they be red like crimson, they shall be as wool." Then Jesus said, "Come unto me, all ye that labour and are heavy laden, and I will give you rest" (Matt. 11:28). Again, He says, "Him that cometh to me I will in no wise cast out" (John 6:37).

God used forty men to write the Bible. John, the beloved apostle, was the last. He was in exile on the Isle of Patmos, where God used him to write the Revelation. John was just about to close the book when God seemed to say, "Wait a minute, John, don't close the book yet. Don't write the last 'Amen' until I give one more urgent invitation to sinners." And here is that invitation in my text today, "And the Spirit and the bride say, Come. And let him that heareth say, Come. And let him that is athirst come. And whosoever will, let him take the water of life freely."

Often on the final night of a revival, when the last stanza of the invitation has been sung, I have said, "Let us go back and sing one more stanza and give someone just one more chance to be saved." So God says here, "Don't close the book, John, until once more I can invite sinners to come for salvation." Maybe God is inviting you today. Maybe He is giving you one more opportunity to come to Christ.

I. WHO INVITES THE SINNERS TO COME?

1. *The Holy Spirit invites.* The first work of the Holy Spirit in the human heart is to convict men of sin and point them to the Lamb of God. It is He who brings about repentance and faith which culminate in our salvation. Those who have been saved can remember how the Spirit of God caused them to see their sin and turn to Christ. If you hear a sermon which causes you to acknowledge that you are a lost sinner, and which makes you feel that you ought to come to Christ, you can know that this is the work of the Holy Spirit.

When Jesus met Paul on the Damascus Road, He said to Paul, "It is hard for thee to kick against the pricks." What were these pricks? Like a sharp pin pricking the flesh the Holy Spirit has been pricking Paul. Often He brought to Paul's mind the face of Stephen, dying for Christ, and his face shining with a heavenly light. He couldn't get away from these pricks.

You who are unsaved have had these same sharp blows on your conscience. You remember your father's faith, your mother's death, the promise you made to them. You remember that when another loved one died, you promised God then that you would live for Him. But you haven't kept that promise. You recall how God has blessed you over the years and how you said, "I ought to be a different man." Yes, today the Holy Spirit touches us in many ways. But remember this. He said, "My Spirit shall not always strive with man." Someday He may lift His hand from your conscience and let you go to hell.

2. *The church of Christ invites.* The "bride" invites you. This is the church of the Lord Jesus Christ now on earth. Surely every true church, every branch of the "bride" is calling out sinners. This is the primary mission of the church. We do many things in and through the church, some which possibly we ought not to do. But the chief task of the church is to win souls and everything we do should have the winning of souls as its ultimate aim. All of us cannot preach or sing or teach, but every Christian should have a part in the winning of souls. Yes, the church, Christ's bride, invites you to come.

3. *The heavenly city invites.* In the Revelation the heavenly city is described as coming down out of heaven. And that city calls us to enter into its portals. There is a hunger in every soul for the rest and peace and joy that can be found only in that city.

> O land of rest, for
>   thee I sigh!
> When will the moment
>   come
> When I shall lay my
>   armor by
> And dwell in peace
>   at home?

We sing about the promised land, the land where there are no disappointments, the land where we never grow old.

We sing of "Jerusalem the Golden" and "Swing Low, Sweet Chariot." People want to go where there is no poverty, no sickness, no death, no sorrow, no tears, no broken hearts and broken homes. Well, such a place is calling, calling, calling us to come to Jesus, so that someday we might live in that wonderful home.

The pauper can come through Christ into that city and become a king. The outcast can have fellowship with Abraham and David and Paul. The sinner can become a saint; the drunkard can become sober; the vile can become pure. Yes, the heavenly city calls you to come to Christ.

4. *Every hearer is to invite.* "Let him that heareth say, Come." The Holy Spirit calls, the church calls, the heavenly home calls. Now God says to every one who hears, "You take up the message, also, and broadcast it to the world."

I heard the message when I was a boy. It broke my heart and made me conscious of my sin and my lost condition. But the message also gave me hope as it pointed me to the Lamb of God who would take away my sin. And I came to Him and He put a new song in my heart. Now I love to tell the story of Jesus and His love. I am thankful that He called me to preach and has given me the privilege of sharing this story over the many years.

We sing about the Promised Land and ask the question, "Oh, who will come and go with me? I am bound for the Promised Land." Are you going? Are you on the way to heaven? Then tell someone else. You'll become a happier and stronger Christian.

A man boarded a train in Chicago. Soon a burly-looking man came in and sat down beside him. When the train pulled out this man who had gotten on last pulled out a Bible and read it for a while. Soon he closed the Bible and said to the other man, "It's a wonderful day, isn't it?" The other man agreed that it was. Then the man said, "There are some fine crops in this section of the country" and the other man said, "Yes, very fine crops." Then said the man, "God is good to give these people such fine crops, isn't He?"

The other man did not reply so this man said, "You didn't reply. Aren't you a Christian?" "No, sir," he answered. So the burly man read a few verses of Scripture and said, "Why not bow your head on the seat right now and let me pray for you?"

In telling about it later the other man said, "Before I knew it I had bowed my head. That man's arm was around me and he was praying for me. When I lifted my head I was a saved man. I had invited Jesus to come into my heart. When we arrived at the station and he started out, I remembered that I did not know who he was. I rushed to the door and shouted, 'What is your name?' He answered in just one word, 'Moody'." He was one man who believed in passing the invitation along.

II. Who Are Those Who Are Invited?

1. *Those who are thirsty are invited.* "Let him that is athirst come." This means everyone who is dissatisfied with life and its pleasures, everyone who is tired of sin, everyone who wants peace in his heart. Zacchaeus, who climbed a tree to see Jesus, was thirsty. The publican who cried out, "God be merciful to me, a sinner," was thirsty. The sinful woman at the well was thirsty. And the world is full of thirsty people today. The trouble is that they are trying to quench that thirst at the wells of the world, wells that can never satisfy.

A chaplain friend of mine said that one day a sailor came into the chaplain's office and talked to a chaplain at the next desk. The boy was in tears. He told this chaplain that he was under deep conviction and needed help. But that chaplain could not give him the right kind of help. He said, "Just do your naval duties, go to chapel and read your Bible. But don't pray so much. You are just trying to escape reality."

When the boy left my chaplain friend said that he could hardly wait to follow him outside to talk to him. He took the boy out back of the chapel, told him about the cleansing blood and the saving grace of Jesus and soon the boy was saved and went on his way rejoicing. He had been thirsty and hungry for Christ.

A certain lady advertised for a maid. She secured a young woman who proved to be a good worker. The woman came to love her and depend on her. In the afternoons when there was no work to be done, the maid would sit by the fire with a Bible in her lap. She would look at the Bible for a long time, then she would look up as if she were listening for a voice from heaven. One day the maid seemed quite blue and depressed, so the lady asked her to tell her what troubled her. And she said, "I'se got a misery, I can't read." Do you see the hunger there? The poor girl couldn't read the Bible, but she felt that there was something in it to help her and she longed for that help. She was thirsting for God.

I can imagine that a group of men are lost in the desert. They stumble about, seeking water. Their tongues are hanging out. They are gasping for breath; some of them fall by the wayside. Then one of them sees a hollow place, with the sun glistening on the water. They rush to the place and find a spring of sparkling water. They throw themselves down and drink and drink until they are satisfied. Out in the desert, we are told, it is a precious privilege to find drinking water when one is almost dying of thirst. Physical thirst is bad, but spiritual thirst is worse. But you don't have to stumble about, seeking a fountain. That fountain is nearby. Christ Himself is the water of life. Come and drink of Him. He satisfies every quest of the human soul.

2. "Whosoever will" is invited. This is the same "whosoever will" that we find in John 3:16. It is an invitation extended and salvation offered to anyone and everyone. I remember seeing a strange ad during World War II. It said, "Do not come to San Francisco. There is no room for you." At that time it was hard to find a vacant house in any city. But Jesus says, "There is plenty of room for you. In my Father's house are many mansions." The gates of heaven are never shut. "Whosoever will" may come.

Is your heart as black as the pits of hell? God loves you and invites you to come. Are you a drunkard? Have you been unfaithful to your marriage vows? Are you a slave to vile habits? Let me assure you that God still loves you and invites you to come. "Whosoever" includes everyone, black, white, yellow, brown or red, rich or poor, high or low. God loves you and holds His arms wide open in loving invitation for you to come to Him through His beloved Son.

3. *Those who will to be saved are invited.* If in your heart you will to drink of the water of life, you are invited to come and be saved.

Dr. M. F. Ham was a great evangelist of another day. He held a revival in Corpus Christi, Texas. The president of the largest bank in the town was a great leader, but his leadership was in a sinful and worldly direction. He attended the revival one night and came under deep conviction for sin. The next morning he phoned Dr. Ham and asked him to ride out in the country with him. When Dr. Ham got in the car the man said, "You certainly hit me last night." As they rode through the town he said, "The people will certainly be surprised to see me riding with a preacher." They stopped by the side of the road far out in the country and Dr. Ham was able to lead the man to Christ. That night he came to the platform to give his testimony. He said, "You people have called me a leader, but from now on I am a follower, a follower of Jesus Christ."

Yes, if you will to leave the old life and follow Jesus, you, too, can be saved.

III. What Is the Invitation?

1. *It is to take the water of life.* Christ provides the water. He offers it to you, but it is up to you to take it. When you are desperately ill and the doctor offers you medicine, you take it or you die. When you are sick in sin and the Great Physician offers you the only remedy for sin, you take it or you die. If you will partake of this water your sins will be

forgiven, your heart will be changed, you will be born into the family of God, you will partake of the divine nature, you will have a daily companion, you will be headed for heaven instead of hell.

A man who was seventy-one years of age held up his hand for prayer in a revival service. Later the preacher said to him, "Do you believe?" The man replied, "I have heard the Gospel before, but I don't exactly understand what you mean by believing." The preacher said, "God furnishes the Saviour, you furnish the sinner. When the sinner trusts the Saviour, he is saved." The man smiled and said, "I can certainly furnish the sinner if God will furnish the Saviour." He claimed Christ and was gloriously saved.

God has done all that is necessary for our salvation. The transaction was completed on Calvary's cross long ago. If you accept His Son, eternal life will be yours.

2. *This water is free.* "Let him take the water of life freely." If you have money on this earth you can stay at the best hotels, you can eat the most expensive food, wear the finest clothes, ride in the highest-priced cars and on the largest jet planes. But you can get to heaven without money and without price. God is not trying to sell you anything. He is trying to give you salvation and eternal life.

Each spring young men and young women go up to a college platform and receive their diplomas, their degrees, the honors they have won. Sometimes the diploma will have on it the words "cum laude" or "magna cum laude" or "summa cum laude." Now this is right and proper. They have worked hard and they have earned these awards. But you don't get salvation that way. You don't work for it; it is free. Heaven is free, eternal life is free, Christ is free to all who come to Him. On the tree of Calvary He purchased our salvation. Now He says "Here it is. It's free. I gladly give to you."

Dr. L. G. Broughton was at one time pastor of the Baptist Tabernacle of Atlanta. A certain man who was a gambler and a liquor dealer applied to the City council for a license to sell liquor near the church. Dr. Broughton went before the council and opposed the granting of the license. The man was there and he became intensely angry at the preacher. The license was refused. One day one of Dr. Broughton's deacons came to him and said, "That liquor man swears that he will kill you if he ever sees you again."

Six weeks later Dr. Broughton went in to his study at the church and found that man sitting there before the fire. He was filled with apprehension. He didn't know what to expect. But the man said, "Dr. Broughton, let's get right down to business. I went home last night and my little girl was on her knees, saying her prayers. I heard her say, 'Oh, Lord, bless my daddy and save him, please.' Then I remembered my mother's prayers back in Virginia when I was a boy. She was the best mother that ever lived. Just think, the boy she used to pray for has sunk so low he can't even get a liquor license. I have come to ask you to kneel and pray with me and not to leave me until I am saved."

After Dr. Broughton had read the great salvation Scriptures to him, both of them went down on their knees. The preacher prayed; the man gave his heart to Christ and arose from his knees, a new man in Christ Jesus. Before the man left he said, "Dr. Broughton, I have three friends who have been in with me in my gambling schemes. I want to see them saved." In a few weeks, through the witness of this new Christian, these men also had come to know the Saviour.

Oh, what a Saviour we have! He can save the highest and he can save the lowest. He invites you to come to Him today. I have talked to you about the last invitation in the Bible. It could be the last invitation for you, also. Will you accept it?

6

GOD'S PEOPLE IN A GODLESS WORLD

Philippians 1:8-11

The Apostle Paul had a true pastor's heart. He would stay for a while in a certain place, build a church there, then go on to another task. But he never forgot the churches he had left in these places. He wrote many wonderful letters to them and he always prayed for them. In writing to the church at Philippi he tells them that he is praying for four things to happen to them.

He wants their love to abound more and more. He wants them to approve the things that are excellent. He wants them to serve God with sincerity. He wants them to be filled with the fruits of righteousness. As Paul thought of his favorite church, let us think of our church and its needs. The Philippian church lived in a godless generation, and so does ours. We must face the facts. There are thousands of unsaved people around us, people who are living without God and without hope. Then we must admit that the average church member is not living at his best for Christ. His Christianity makes little impression on the outside world. Like the lost man, he often lives as if there were no God.

Paul wanted the Philippian church to make an impression for Christ on a godless generation. We want our church to make an impression for Christ on the godless generation in which we live. Let us think of five vital things which we will need in order to effectively influence the world.

I. We Need to Live More Consecrated Christian Lives

The mere fact that our names are on the church roll does not influence the outside world. They must see that we are different, that something has happened within us that has changed us. In New Testament days the people took note of the believers, that they had been with Jesus. Why did they notice this? Because these people were different — their lives were different from others. If we expect to impress the world, our conversion must have been a thing that changed us and made us better people.

Now this is not always an instantaneous change. Sometimes a gradual change begins with conversion and increases in power from day to day. We call that "growing in grace." It is brought about by prayer, by the study of God's Word, by a faithfulness to Christian duty, by a daily walk with Christ. But many of our people are not growing in grace. They are not any better or stronger Christians now than they were on the day of their conversion. Some of them are not even as strong as they were on that day.

They have been saved, but that is all. They never grow in grace, never influence others for Christ, never learn the joy of true service, never know the thrill of a daily walk with Christ. They never show an appreciation for Christ in their lives. They will come to the end of the way, and when they face Him they won't be able to say that they have done one thing for the One who has done all things for them.

Pause just a moment. Ask yourself if you are that kind of a Christian. If you are I plead with you right now to turn from such a life and resolve that from now on you are going to be a Christian who counts for Christ.

A certain girl gave her heart to Christ when she was a teen-ager. Later she married an unsaved man. This was a mistake but she kept on living for Jesus every day. The years passed. Her husband cared nothing for Christ. He would never even attend church. But the broken-hearted mother remained true to her Lord, living a deeply consecrated life. Several children were born and that sweet mother taught them to love and follow Jesus.

Finally, disease set its grasp upon her and she was dying. Calling her husband to her bedside, she said, "My dear, I have tried to be a faithful wife. I do hope that you will receive Christ as your Saviour and bring the little ones up in the right way. I want all of you to meet me in heaven some day." She then called the children to the bedside and said to them, "I have taught you to look to Jesus; I have trained you to walk with Him. I hope you'll always be faithful to the Lord."

After the funeral at the church, her body was taken to the cemetery for burial. The husband and children stood by and saw the last clod of earth fall upon the casket. Then they went home with heavy hearts. It seemed that all the light had gone out of the sky for them. That night the father put the children to bed and sat by the fireside, thinking. Soon he heard the little boy sobbing. Going into the bedroom he said, "What's the matter, Johnny, are you hungry?" "No, sir," he answered. "Are you thirsty?" "No, sir." The father said, "What is the trouble, son?" And the little boy said, "Papa, mother used to get all of us around her knees at night. She would read to us about Jesus, then she would put her hands on our head and pray for us. You put us to bed without our prayers." Later, when the father gave his testimony, he said, "I couldn't stand it any longer. I got the children up, read them a few verses from my wife's Bible, then I fell on my knees beside the children. I told God that I wanted Christ to be my Saviour, that I would give Him my heart and life, and that I wanted Him to use me to train my children for the Lord."

The man became a faithful Christian. Why? Because of the consecrated life of a good woman. Oh, that's our great need today. Our lives would be different. We would make some impression on others, if only we lived consecrated Christian lives.

Sometime ago I visited a woman who was a member of

our church. Her husband was not a Christian. But this wo-man never darkened the door of the church, never gave a penny to the Lord's work, and was completely indifferent to spiritual things. I came away saying, "If that woman had lived a faithful life for Christ, she would have influenced her husband toward salvation long ago."

I believe that the average person, if he lives faithfully for Christ, as all Christians should, can make an impression on family and friends that they can not shake off.

II. WE NEED THE POWER THAT COMES FROM A DEEPER DEVOTIONAL LIFE

I am afraid that the only time some church members hear a verse of Scripture is when they hear it read from the pulpit on Sunday. And they let hours and days go by without prayer. But we can never have any power to influence anyone else for Christ unless we spend some time alone with God. The day should begin in prayer. As we wake up and think of the duties of the day, we should pray. As we sit down to our meals we should lift our hearts and voices in thanksgiving to God. As we go to work we should pray that God would help us in our work and in every contact we make. As we face the decisions of the day we should pray for wisdom. As we retire for the night we should thank God for the blessings of the day and ask God to forgive the sins we have committed.

Here is a strange fact. We know God answers prayer; we read that in the Bible. But more than that, we have ex-perienced answered prayer. Yet we go along through life, starving our souls, never stopping to pray for help that He alone can give us.

> O what peace we often forfeit,
> O what needless pain we bear,
> All because we do not carry
> Everything to God in prayer!

It is said that Martin Luther often spent from four to six hours in prayer on some days. The busier he was, the more time he spent in prayer. We should be ashamed that we pray so little. As I look across the years and think of the many times when God has answered my prayers, I am ashamed that I have not prayed more. Jesus said that "men ought always to pray, and not to faint." Paul said that we are to "pray without ceasing."

A woman called a theater one morning and told the manager that she had attended the theater the night before and had lost a pearl necklace in one of the boxes. She said that the necklace was worth $1,000 but was valued more highly as a family heirloom. The manager told her to hold the telephone while he checked to see if he could find the necklace. He did find it and went back to the phone to tell her so, but she had hung up and didn't call back. That is like some of us. We pray, and when the answer doesn't come immediately, we quit praying. But our lives should be lives of prayer.

In every church there are members who never attend church, who never give, and who ignore the church year by year. What would happen if these people fell on their knees and prayed every day? They would see themselves as sinners before God. They would confess their sins and find their way back to God's house. That's what prayer would do for them. But they go their worldly ways. They have absolutely no spiritual power, and never influence anyone for good.

A Texas church found a couple who lived a few blocks from the church and began visiting them. The wife was a backslidden church member, and the husband was not a Christian. The church members visited them once or twice and the couple became absolutely insulting to them. One day at noon this woman looked out of her window. She saw her postman as he sat down on the curb to eat his lunch. Before he ate he took off his hat, bowed his head and gave thanks. This touched her heart and set her to thinking. She told her husband about the postman and he, too, was impressed. He said that if the postman could sit on the curb and give thanks, they ought to give thanks in the home. On Sunday they went to church and heard a moving sermon. When the invitation was given the woman went forward to transfer her letter and the man confessed Christ as his Saviour. The following Sunday his father and mother and sister made a confession of faith and another sister and brother-in-law joined the church by letter.

What started it all? A faithful man who loved God stopped to pray, not knowing the effect this simple act would have on an entire family.

God's people live in a godless world. Evil is all around us. But we have two wonderful things to help us. We have the open Bible, through which God speaks to us. And we have the privilege of prayer, whereby we speak to God. Through these things power comes to us, power to influence others for Christ.

III. We Need to Develop the Right Concepts of a New Testament Church

A New Testament church must be one founded by Jesus Christ Himself. It must be one founded in New Testament times and in the New Testament land. There are many practices in some churches today which were not mentioned in the Bible. There's the idea of Lent, practiced by many churches today. A radio commentator recently said, "These are great days for Christians. The forty days of Lent commemorate the forty days which Jesus spent in the wilderness. Many people show their love for Christ by giving up their cigarettes, their candy or their cocktails during this season." But surely if it is wrong to indulge in certain things for these forty days, it is wrong all the year around.

There is the idea of universalism so prevalent in many churches today. They proclaim that all men are the children of God, regardless of their sin or their rejection of Christ. But we are God's children only when we repent of our sins and receive Christ as our personal Saviour and Lord. John 1:12 says, "As many as received him, to them gave he power to become the sons of God, even to them that believe on his name." In our natural state we are not God's children. We are not born as God's children; we must be born again to enter into His family.

Then there's the idea of "purgatory." The teaching here is that when men die, even though they be the best of Christians, they must go to some intermediate state and have all their sins burned away. This is against all Bible doctrine. The Scriptures teach us plainly that Christ has already done enough to save us from all sin and to take us to heaven at the end of the way. If Jesus paid it all, we don't have to pay it again. There is no room in Bible doctrine for purgatory. We have no right to subtract from or add to the New Testament pattern.

Oh, the great need today is for us to study the Bible and go by its teachings instead of our own finite conceptions. Christ planted the church here so that Christians would have a medium through which to carry out the Great Commission and to do His work in the world. When we have the right concept of the church we will love it as Christ did. We will line up with it wherever we are and we'll give our best service through it.

An old man went to church every time there was a service. Yet he was stone deaf. He could not hear the music of the choir nor the message of the preacher. A scoffer said to him, "Why do you go to church every Sunday? You can't hear anything that goes on." And he replied, "I want my neighbors to know whose side I am on." If we love the Lord we'll be faithful to His church and the world will know where we stand. And our religion will make some impression upon them.

IV. WE NEED A REVIVAL OF OUR MISSIONARY ZEAL

Our missionaries stay for years on a foreign field, then when they come home their hearts are heavy. They see us with our beautiful buildings and fine equipment and they are saddened because we do so little to make Christ known around the world. I remember that when we were in a large building program in El Paso we raised our mission giving every year. And in His own way God saw to it that we didn't suffer. All of our needs were supplied.

It takes two wings to enable a bird to fly. And I believe our love for Christ ought to fly on two wings, our gifts for the work at home and our gifts for the work abroad.

Because Jesus died for us and saved us, we owe a debt that we can never repay, even if we spent twenty-four hours a day working for Him. But we can try to repay that debt by witnessing for Him in every way possible. Listen to how the great apostle felt about it, "I am debtor both to the Greeks, and to the Barbarians; both to the wise, and to the unwise. So, as much as in me is, I am ready to preach the gospel to you that are at Rome also. For I am not ashamed of the gospel of Christ: for it is the power of God unto salvation to every one that believeth; to the Jew first, and also to the Greek" (Rom. 1:14-16).

Now when we speak of missionary zeal, we mean personal efforts to win those around us and personal gifts to be used in sending others around the world to tell of the saving grace of Christ.

A preacher tells about a creek that ran near his old home. The only way to cross it was to "ford" it. Sometimes as a result of the heavy rains the creek overflowed its banks. One day when the creek was high a man tried to go across in his buggy. The water swept against the buggy, the horse became unhitched, and the man was thrown into a deep pool. Another man saw his predicament and pulled him out safely. As soon as he recovered his breath he gasped out that there was another man in the pool and he rushed out to rescue this man. Just as the man who had been rescued remembered someone else who was drowning, so we who have been rescued from the flames of hell should remember that others are on the downward path. And we ought to be anxious that they be rescued, also.

V. WE NEED TO REMEMBER THAT CHRIST MAY COME BACK ANY MINUTE

Now the Bible teaches us that His coming is imminent. At any minute he might break through the blue and come in the air. This thought ought to be the supreme incentive to cause us to give Him our best. If we realize that He might come at any minute and that then we must give Him an account of our lives there are certain things we should be doing.

We should be living more consecrated Christian lives. We should seek a deeper and more meaningful devotional life. We should seek to have the right concept of Christ's New Testament church. And we should pray for a revival of personal soul-winning and world-wide missionary zeal.

Here is a boy who loves his father devotedly. One day his father gives him a task to perform. He tells the boy that he will return at noon to see how well the boy has done his work. Since the boy wants to please his father he doesn't spend the morning in idleness, but works hard so that he can show his father some good results at noon. Well, friend, we may be nearing the noontime when Christ will return. So we have no right to waste our time on the things of this world that will die with the setting sun. Let us work the works of Him who saved us, for the time draws nigh when no man can work.

Oh, in the light of the past, as we think of the cross and all Christ has done for us, I call upon you to be more faithful to Christ and His church. And in the light of the future, as we think of His return and all the wonderful things waiting for us, I again plead with you to be more faithful in all things and in all ways to Christ and His church.

The wife of a prominent Kentucky man had a nervous breakdown. Her mind became almost a blank. The specialists were called in but they could do nothing for her. They advised her husband to take her to the Rocky Mountains where she might become aroused and be her old self again. He closed his business and their home and took her to a beautiful mountain resort, where all was quiet and peaceful. He served her with the most devoted affection, but never one time did she give any hint that she even knew him. All he received in return for all his devotion was a blank stare.

Then he took her to the sunny shores of Florida. Day by day he walked arm in arm with her, seeking in every way to arouse her. One Sunday afternoon she lay down on the couch and dropped off into a deep sleep. Her breathing was long and regular. Her husband sat beside her, stroked her forehead, kissed her cheek and prayed that she would come back to him. Finally she opened her eyes, looked up at her husband with the old look of love and said, "Where have you been so long?" And with tears of love and gratitude raining down his cheek, he replied, "My darling, I have been right here waiting for you to come back to me."

Friend, don't you see it? God has been waiting for you to respond to His love. Some of you are His children, but you have gone back into the world. He is waiting in love for you to come back. Some of you are unsaved. He is waiting for you to come to Him for salvation and everlasting life.

Won't you hear and heed the voice of the Saviour right now?

7

THE MOST UNPOPULAR SUBJECT IN THE WORLD

Romans 6:11-23

There are many unpopular subjects that a preacher might use, but today I want to talk about the most unpopular subject in the world — Sin. The word has in it the hiss of a serpent. It ruins lives in this world and condemns souls to the everlasting fires in the world to come.

Let us ask and answer four questions about sin:

    I. What Is Sin?
    II. Where Did Sin Come From?
    III. What Does Sin Do To People?
    IV. How Can You Get Rid of Sin?

I. WHAT IS SIN?

Let's look at the Bible definitions of sin.

1. *Sin is "transgression of the law"* (I John 3:4). Transgression means "to go across." You ride down the street and you come to a traffic light. The light is red. You know that you will violate the law if you drive through it, but you go right ahead and cross against the light. You have violated the law. Now God's law is our standard, our red light. That law is straight. If you go across it, if you disobey or disregard it, you have sinned.

Man's law is fashioned after God's law. His law says that we are not to steal or kill, man's law says the same. Man's laws are founded on God's Ten Commandments. When we break God's laws, we have sinned.

2. *Sin is rebellion against God.* The prodigal son cried out, "I have sinned against heaven and in thy sight." David said, "Against thee, thee only have I sinned." Sin is against others, it hurts others, it breaks the hearts of those whom we love. But primarily it is against God. David sinned greatly against Bathsheba and Uriah, but he recognized that his sin was first of all against God. Every sin is a blow to the heart of God, every sinner is a rebel.

3. *Sin is the omission of good.* "Therefore to him that knoweth to do good, and doeth it not, to him it is sin" (James 4:17). God places certain responsibilities on every one of us. When we neglect our duty to Him, we are guilty of sin.

Many of our people have been saved in a certain location and have joined a nearby church. Later they moved to another state and left their church membership behind. Soon they drifted away from the church and from the Lord. I say that they are living in sin, because they know to do good, but do it not.

When one deliberately does wrong, that is the sin of commission. When one refuses to do that which is right, that is the sin of omission.

4. *A bad spirit is sin.* A wrong attitude on your part toward someone else is sinful. And right here is where so many Christians sin greatly. Our churches are full of people who let hatred, malice, envy and jealousy rankle in their hearts. These people would be horrified even to think of stealing or drinking or committing adultery, yet those who have the wrong attitude toward others are just as guilty of sin as if they had committed these grosser evils.

5. *Unbelief is sin.* "He that believeth on the Son hath everlasting life: and he that believeth not the Son shall not see life, but the wrath of God abideth on him" (John 3:36).

The greatest sin is not murder nor adultery nor theft. Many of those who have committed these sins have found forgiveness and salvation in Christ. But if you go to your grave without Christ there will be no hope for you. Unbelief is the damning sin, the one that dooms men to hell. Unbelief leads all other sins — it is the cause of all other sins. The sins of men spring from a heart of unbelief.

II. WHERE DID SIN COME FROM?

1. *It came from Satan.* He was the original sinner. In heaven he had a high place among the angels. It appears that he was next to Jesus Himself in authority and glory. But he was not satisfied. He wanted the first place. He wanted to topple God off His throne and take His place as ruler of the universe. The time came when he rebelled against God and God cast him out of heaven. Then he came down to earth and brought sin with him.

Look at the tragedy in the Garden of Eden. God had made a wonderful world and He put Adam and Eve in the most beautiful spot in that world. He surrounded them with every good thing. He walked and talked with them every day. Then one day Satan slipped in and tempted that first couple. They fell into sin and were consequently banished from Eden. And when they were driven out of the Garden, Satan laughed, for he had accomplished his mission. Sin had entered into the human race and Adam and Eve reached up and pulled all of future humanity down into sin with them.

And, oh, the tragic results of that sin. The germ of sin which entered the veins of our first parents has been passed on down through generation after generation until it now lives and operates in us. Satan brought sin into the world. Man, made in the image of God, fell before temptation.

2. *It comes out of a sinful heart.* "For out of the heart proceed evil thoughts, murders, adulteries, fornications, thefts, false witnesses, blasphemies" (Matt. 15:19). Yes, sin comes out of a sinful heart, but Satan placed it there.

A Sunday school teacher asked a class of girls the question, "Do we have anything that we have not received from God?" And one little girl answered wisely, "Yes, our sins." She was right. Sin originated with Satan and it is he who tempts us today.

III. WHAT DOES SIN DO TO PEOPLE?

Let us look at some Bible examples, showing us the consequence of sin.

1. *Achan and his sin.* Joshua had just led Israel into the Promised Land. He told his men not to touch any of the spoils out of the city of Jericho. Now there was a soldier in his army named Achan. He saw some things that he coveted: a suit of clothes, 200 shekels of silver and a wedge of gold. He stole these things and hid them in his tent. The next day Joshua sent a small army against the weak city of Ai. He felt that the city could be taken easily. But to his dismay his army was utterly defeated. Knowing that something was wrong, he went before God and the Lord said to him, "There is sin in the camp. Get it out if you expect Me to be with you."

The next day Joshua called the people together and it was learned that Achan was the guilty party. Being confronted with his sin, Achan fell before Joshua and confessed his sin. Now let's see what sin did to Achan, as recorded in Joshua 7:24, 25, "And Joshua, and all Israel with him, took Achan the son of Zerah, and the silver, and the garment, and the wedge of gold, and his sons, and his daughters, and his oxen, and his asses, and his sheep, and his tent, and all that he had: and they brought them unto the valley of Achor. And Joshua said, Why hast thou troubled us? the Lord shall trouble thee this day. And all Israel stoned him with stones, and burned them with fire, after they had stoned them with stones."

That night I walk down into the valley. My nostrils catch the scent of burning flesh and I see a heap of stones. Then I remember that twenty-four hours earlier this man and his family were alive and happy; now they are gone. Oh, Achan, that's what sin did to you. "The wages of sin is death."

2. *Saul and his sin.* There came a time when Israel cried out for a king. God decided to let them have one. He gave them Saul, a big man, a man a head taller than any of them. He started off well, asking God to help him in everything. He won many victories and became very popular. Then he came to the time when he felt that he didn't need God, that he was strong enough in himself. He disobeyed God; he plunged ahead and God rejected him. He was so far away from God that he called upon a witch for advice.

Then one day in a fierce battle he saw that all was lost. He knew that God had forsaken him because he had forsaken God. So he took a sword, fell on it and committed suicide. There he lies, a sword sticking through his body. He could have been a great king, but sin brought him down to death. If he could speak he would say, "The wages of sin is death."

There are many men like Saul today. They start off in a humble way; they ask God to help them. Soon they have gone up the ladder and all things are theirs. Then they come to the time when they feel that they don't need God, so they cast Him aside, only to wake up some day and find that God has turned His back upon them.

3. *David and his sin.* Sin loves a shining mark. It cut David down — the man who wrote the 23rd Psalm — the man after God's own heart. One day when there were no battles to be fought, David lolled upon the housetop. He looked over into the courtyard next door and saw a beautiful woman taking a bath, and he coveted her for himself. "Who is this woman?" he asked. And the answer came, "She is Uriah's wife." But despite the fact that he knew she was another man's wife, he took her for himself and lived in sin with her. But this was not all. Sin grows. David called in Uriah's commanding officer and told him to put Uriah in the hottest part of the next battle, so that he would certainly be killed. So while the king sat in his luxurious palace and enjoyed the presence of Uriah's wife, poor old Uriah died a

bloody death on the field of battle. Then David took Bath-sheba, Uriah's wife, to himself and married her.

Is that all there is to the story? Will David go scot-free? Will God overlook David's sin? Listen to 2 Samuel 11:27, "But the thing that David had done displeased the Lord." And when God is displeased He does something about it. What did He do? We read that from that time the sword never departed from David's house. (1) The child that was born to this unholy union died in infancy, breaking David's heart. (2) One of David's sons sinned against his half-sister in the way that David had sinned. (3) Then another son killed the son who had committed this sin. (4) Finally David's favorite son, Absalom, raised up an army against David and was himself killed.

When the messenger brought the news of Absalom's death to David, his heart really broke. We find here one of the most touching scenes in the Bible. We see the old father climbing the stairs to the solitude of his room. We hear him weeping and sobbing out his sorrow, "O my son Absalom, my son, my son Absalom! would God I had died for thee, O Absalom, my son, my son."

"David," we ask, "does sin pay?" And he answers, "No, my sin brought death to all of my happiness. The wages of sin is indeed death."

But David was a man after God's own heart, so there was a difference in him and a man who did not know God. When he was confronted with his sin, he confessed his guilt, turned away from his sin and cried out to God for forgiveness. And God heard his cry, forgave his sin and restored to David the joy of His salvation.

Now here's another difference in David and others. He sinned and was punished for his sin in this world. When the unbeliever sins, God reserves the punishment of hell for him. Yes, "the wages of sin is death."

4. *Judas and his sin.* There was another man, a man who walked with Jesus for three and a half years. He heard the wonderful things that Jesus said; he saw the marvelous things

He did; he felt the impact of His gracious and tremendous spirit. Then one day the enemies of Jesus called him in to a conference. "Judas," they said, "deliver Jesus to us and we'll give you thirty pieces of silver." He agreed to the bargain. That night Jesus was praying in Gethsemane. When He came from the place of prayer, Judas stepped up and kissed Him on the cheek. Then Jesus' enemies arrested Him and led Him to His death.

But even Judas, who loved money, could not enjoy the silver he received. Remorse overcame him, so he went back to the enemies of Christ and said, "Let's rue the bargain, I have betrayed innocent blood." And they laughed him to scorn. What did Judas do then? He went out into the garden, threw a rope over a limb and hanged himself, and fell dead at the foot of the tree.

Let's take a walk in the moonlight. Under a tree we see a crumpled, broken figure, with the rays of the moon falling upon it. It is the body of the betrayer. "Judas," we ask, "does sin pay?" The dumb lips cannot answer us, but the facts cry out, "The wages of sin is death."

I'll tell you what sin does to people. It brings unhappiness, trouble, poverty and misery into this world. And if you die in your sin without Jesus Christ as your Saviour, it will bring suffering and hell throughout all eternity.

5. *Jesus and our sin.* Let me tell you what sin did to another life. God had an only Son, perfect and holy. He came down into the world and lived here more than thirty-three years. He never had a sinful thought; He never spoke a sinful word; no sinful act ever came from His hands. And what happened at the end? Just go with me to Calvary. There we see three crosses on a hill. On the outside crosses two criminals are dying, on the central cross hangs the Son of God. Why is He dying there? What crime has He committed? What wrong has He done?

He is dying because of sin. Not His sin, but ours. Our sin sent Him to the cross. Our sin pressed the crown of thorns down on His brow. Our sin lashed His back. Our sin formed the cross. Our sin drove the nails in His hands and feet and thrust the spear into His side.

Oh, if sin is so evil as to reach up into heaven and pluck the Father's own Son out of His bosom and bring Him into a sinful world where cruel men will slay Him, we ought to hate sin with all of our being.

A certain lady went out into her flower garden to gather roses. She saw one especially beautiful rose on the back side of a bush and leaned far over the bush to cut that rose. As she did so a small black snake in the bush fell on her arm and wrapped itself around that arm. She ran from the garden, screaming, and shook off the snake. She ran into the house in hysterics and it was hours before she could gain her composure. After that time she came to hate the entire serpent race. She never wanted to look upon a snake, even if it was dead.

That's the way we ought to feel about sin. It put our Saviour to death and we ought to hate it. Yes, your sin and mine killed the Son of God.

IV. How Can We Get Rid of Sin?

Men today try to get rid of sin in various ways. Some try to cover it up, but you can't hide it from God. Some try to deny it, but the Bible says, "All have sinned and come short of the glory of God." Some make excuses and say, "All of us are human, so I am not to blame." But God says that we must give an account for every evil deed.

There is only one right thing to do about sin. We must acknowledge that we have sinned, turn away from it, repent of it and confess it to God. We must turn it all over to Jesus Christ, the great sin-bearer.

Am I speaking to a Christian who has sinned? Have you allowed something to come between you and God? Have you backslidden into the world? You can never be happy or useful if anything stands between you and the Lord.

A burglar once robbed a house by the seashore, a house

that was not occupied during the winter months. The evidence showed later that he had brought all the plunder into the living room and had placed it on the floor, then had sat down to rest. On the mantle there was a small statue of Christ, so the burglar turned it to the wall, so that the Saviour could not look upon his evil deeds. But this was his undoing. He left his fingerprints on the little statue, was arrested and found guilty. Don't be deceived. You can't hide your sin from God. There's only one thing to do about it. Turn away from it, be done with it. Leave your sin and turn back to God.

Sinner friend, man without Christ, what are you going to do about your sin? Are you going to hold on to it and let it take you down to hell?

Centuries ago a prominent man named Theotimus lived in drunkenness and licentiousness. His eyesight began to fail and the doctor told him that he would lose his sight entirely if he did not give up his sinful practices. But he was so wedded to his sin that he cried, "Then farewell, sweet light," held on to his sin and lost his sight. Are you willing to hold on to your sin and give up light and life, God and heaven?

Isaiah says, "Seek ye the Lord while He may be found, call ye upon him while He is near: Let the wicked forsake his way, and the unrighteous man his thoughts: and let him return unto the Lord, and he will have mercy upon him; and to our God, for he will abundantly pardon" (Isa. 55:6, 7).

God's biggest business in the world is saving lost sinners. He gave His only begotten Son for that purpose. He gave us the Bible for that purpose. He sent the Holy Spirit for that purpose. He established the church for that purpose. He calls preachers for that purpose.

God is calling you to repent and turn to Him. Every invitation in the Bible is a personal one to you. Every church steeple is pointing you to God. Every sermon is God's call to you. Now you don't have to answer His call. He will not force Himself on you. But, oh, the folly and tragedy of turning Him down. If you live without Christ you will end up in hell. Then you will call on God and there will be no answer.

Some shepherds once saw an eagle soar out from a crag. The great bird flew far up into the sky, then the shepherds saw it waver in its flight. One wing drooped, then another, then the poor eagle fell to its death. The shepherds went over to the dead eagle and found a tiny serpent embedded in its feathers. The serpent has fastened itself to the eagle while the eagle was on the crag. It had gnawed through the feathers, thrust its fang deep into the eagle's flesh and brought it down to earth.

You may welcome sin into your life and find it sweet for a while. You may fly very high. But finally your sin will bring you crashing down, down to eternal death. Do you want that to be your fate? Of course not. Then come to Jesus before it is too late.

The text says that "the wages of sin is death." But look at the other side, "the gift of God is eternal life through Jesus Christ our Lord." God doesn't sell salvation and heaven, He gives them away. He is waiting now for you to accept His gift.

Dr. George W. Truett was saved in a revival meeting in the mountains of North Carolina. His desk-mate in school was unsaved. On the next to the last night of the meetings the two boys sat together. During the invitation George noticed that his friend was greatly moved, so he leaned over and said, "Jim, won't you go down? I have been saved and it is wonderful. Go down and give your heart to Christ, Jim." But Jim said, "Let me off tonight, George. If I feel this way tomorrow night I will make my surrender." Then George said, "Don't wait, Jim. Do it tonight. I'll walk down the aisle with you." But Jim said, "Not tonight, George, not tonight."

The next day Jim was not in school and he wasn't in the meeting that night. The second day George went to Jim's house to learn where he had been. Jim's mother met George at the door and said, "Didn't you know? Jim came home sick from the revival and now he has pneumonia. The doctor won't allow him to have any company."

George went back every day for seven days, and was not permitted to see his friend. On the eighth day Jim's mother said, "There is no hope for him." George then said, "Let me go in, maybe he'll know me. I want to talk to him about Christ." When George went into the bedroom he found Jim to be delirious. He did not even know George. He just kept on saying, "Not tonight, George, not tonight. I'll give Christ my heart tomorrow night, but not tonight, George." And in a few minutes he went out to meet God.

Oh, friends, men ought not to die like that. They don't have to die like that. Christ is calling, His arms are wide open to receive you and save you. What will you do about it?

8

THE QUESTION FOR EVERY HEART

Matthew 22:42

There are many important questions confronting the man of today. Think of some of them. Where shall I live? In the city or the country? In the north or south or east or west? What career shall I select? What profession must be mine? Whom shall I marry? How can I best rear my children? These are just a few of the scores of questions for men to answer today. But there is one great, important, meaningful universal question facing every man, woman, boy and girl in the world. It is asked by Jesus Himself and every man must answer it. Here it is: "What think ye of Christ?"

You ask a friend, "What do you think of the president or the governor or the mayor?" But these are insignificant questions compared to this great question. What do you think of Jesus, my friend? If you think well of Him, get on His side, give your life to Him, serve Him with all of your energy, follow Him, be faithful to Him unto death. Surely no one can think ill of Him. He is God's Son; He loved you; He died for you; He wants the best for you.

I. WHAT THIS QUESTION IS NOT

1. *The question is not "What think ye of the church?"* Often when we try to confront man with the claims of Christ, they begin to tell us what they think is wrong with the church. But that is not the question. We know that the

church is not perfect. It is composed of human beings and therefore can never be perfect on this side of glory. But it is still the greatest institution on earth. Civilization would perish without its influence. All that is good in our national life comes from it. From whence came our schools, our hospitals, our childrens' homes, our charitable institutions? They grew out of the church and its influence and teachings.

I wish that every church member in the world felt the responsibility to the church that they should. Let us love it, boost it, support it, be faithful to it. But the big question is not, "What think ye of the church?"

2. *The question is not "what think ye of His representatives."* Often when an unsaved person is confronted with the matter of his relationship to God, he points to some Christian who is not what he ought to be and gives that man's life as an excuse for his own indifference to Christ. "Look at that man," he will say. "I live a better life than he does, so why should I change?" Yes, we know that some of Christ's reprentatives live shabby lives, but that is not the question. We are not to judge Christ by His followers.

An American Ambassador to a foreign country may behave very badly, but the citizens of that country should not judge America by that one man's behavior. Benedict Arnold, a great soldier of the United States, betrayed his country, but that doesn't mean that all soldiers are traitors. A banker showed me some counterfeit bills, but that doesn't mean that all money is worthless. Some Christians are sinful and sorry but that doesn't mean that Christ is deficient in any way.

But the best people of all times have been Christians. And although some of them are not what they ought to be, we are not to judge Christ by them. The question is not "What think ye of His representatives?"

3. *The question is not "What think ye of the doctrines of the church?"* A man says, "I don't believe in baptism." But what does that matter if he is not saved? Another man says, "I don't believe in the Lord's Supper." But what does that matter if he is on the way to hell? Another man says, "I

don't believe in your form of church government." But what does that matter if Satan is governing his life?

A condemned man sits in his prison cell awaiting execution. The governor of the state visits him to talk to him about a pardon. But the condemned man begins to complain when he ought to be pleading for his life. He doesn't like the prison food; he doesn't like the clothes they furnish him; he doesn't like his cell. But what do these things matter when his very life is at stake? So the man without Christ is a condemned man. He has no time to argue about the doctrines of the church. It is time for him to cry out to Christ for salvation.

So we see that this question is not an earthly one. It is one God is asking you. He is saying, "Christ is my only begotten Son. I loved you enough to give Him up for you. What do you think of Him? What are you going to do with Him?" When you answer this question correctly, when you settle this matter, all else will come out all right.

II. What Some Others Think of Him

1. *Let us hear first from His enemies.*

(1) *We ask the Pharisees what they thought of Him.* And they answer, "This man receives sinners." What a charge! What an indictment! That's why He came into the world, that's why He loved us. Thank God, He does receive sinners. If He didn't, where would you and I be?

On the cross they said, "He saved others, himself he cannot save." It is true He could not save Himself and save us, also. He had to give Himself to save us. So the testimony of the Pharisees does not condemn Him. He indeed "received sinners." He still does, thank God. So we see that the testimony of the Pharisees does not condemn Him.

(2) *We ask Caiaphas what he thought of Him.* "You were the chief priest, the head of the Sanhedrin. You talked to Him, what did you think of Him?" And he says, "I asked Him if He was the Son of God and He said that He was.

He also said that someday the world would see Him coming in glory and sitting upon a throne." And that is all His bitterest enemy could say against Him.

(3) *We ask Pilate what he thought of Him.* "He was brought before you, governor; you examined Him. What did you think of Him?" And Pilate says in all sincerity, "I could find no fault in Him." And his wife says to him, "Don't have anything to do with hurting this just man." Neither Pilate nor his wife could find anything wrong with Jesus.

Someone has painted a picture of Pilate in hell. When he released Jesus here on earth to be crucified, he washed his hands and said, "I am innocent of the blood of this just man." In this picture we see Pilate in hell, forever washing his hands but never cleansing them. He exchanged the favor of Christ for the favor of men. But he could never say anything against Jesus.

(4) *We ask Judas what he thought of Him.* "You knew Him for over three years, Judas. You heard Him preach — you saw His wonderful miracles — you knew of His beautiful spirit. You sold Him for thirty pieces of silver. What did you think of Him?" And as he throws down the money paid over to him, he cries out, "He is innocent, I have betrayed the innocent blood." Poor Judas! His conscience condemned him, but he couldn't say anything against Jesus.

(5) *We ask the centurion what he thought of Him.* "Captain, you had charge of the soldiers who crucified Him. You and they were acting under orders. You saw them drive those nails in His hands and feet. You saw Him hanging on the cross. You watched Him die. What did you think of Him?" And he answers, "Truly this was the Son of God."

God caused every man who had anything to do with the death of Christ to put a testimony on record that He was indeed the innocent Son of God.

(6) *We ask the thief who died by His side.* "You climbed up the hill of Calvary with Him. You were there when He was lifted up by your side. You saw how He acted. You heard His words. What did you think of Him?" And the

thief says, "I railed upon Him at first and He didn't say a word. Suddenly it flashed upon my mind that this was no mere Man. God seemed to tell me that this was His Son. I begged Him to remember me when He became a King. And He promised to take me straight home to Paradise. Yes, He is God's Son."

(7) *We ask the devils themselves what they thought of Him.* And they give a glowing testimony, saying, "Thou Son of the most High God."

So we take the testimony of all His enemies and put them together and they all witness in favor of Jesus Christ. They all attest to His deity and His power.

2. *Let us hear from His friends.*

(1) *Call John the Baptist.* "John, you were a mighty preacher. When you preached by the River Jordan the cities emptied themselves to come out to hear you. God had chosen you to be His forerunner. What did you think of Him?" And he answers, "Behold the Lamb of God, which taketh away the sin of the world."

(2) *We call Simon Peter.* "Peter, you were His chief disciple. You walked with Him and talked with Him. You knew every intimate detail about Him. What did you think of Him?" And old Peter answers, "He is the Christ, the Son of the Living God. And unto us who believe, He is precious."

(3) *We call the Apostle John.* "John, you loved Him so deeply. You leaned upon His bosom at the Last Supper. You were at Calvary with His mother when He died. What did you think of Him?" And John answers, "I wrote an entire book about Him. He was the Light of the World, the Bright and Morning Star, the Word of God. And sixty-seven years after He died and rose again I heard Him say from heaven, 'Behold, I come quickly.' And I said, 'Even so, come, Lord Jesus.'"

(4) *We call doubting Thomas.* "Thomas, the other disciples told you He had risen from the dead, but you were like so many of us, you didn't believe it. Now what did you

think of Him?" And Thomas says, "I saw Him in the Upper Room and I knew then that they were right. He was indeed alive and standing right there before me. And I fell before Him and cried out, 'My Lord and my God.'"

(5) *We call the people of Decapolis, the Ten Cities.* "You saw His mighty miracles performed in your presence. What did you think of Him?" And they answer, "He hath done all things well."

(6) *We call Saul who became Paul.* "You were His bitter enemy. You persecuted His followers and put them to death. You tried to stamp out His name on the earth. What did you think of Him?" And Paul answers, "I met Him one day on the Damascus Road. He saved me. He turned me about face. I have walked with Him and told people about Him for many years. I'll soon see Him face to face. I have suffered the loss of all things just to know Him. He is my all in all."

(7) *We call the angels of the Lord.* "You saw Him in the bosom of the Father. You saw Him leave heaven. You saw Him come forth as the tiny babe in Bethlehem's stable. What do you think of Him?" And we hear the answer, "Behold, I bring you good tidings of great joy, which shall be to all people. For unto you is born this day in the city of David a Saviour, which is Christ the Lord."

(8) *We call the hosts of heaven, the redeemed of all ages.* And they say, "We are they whose robes have been washed in the blood of the Lamb. Worthy is He to receive power and riches, and wisdom, and strength and honor, and glory and blessing."

(9) *We call the supreme Witness, God the Father.* And we hear Him saying, above the Jordan River, "This is my beloved Son in whom I am well pleased." And on the Mount of Transfiguration we hear Him saying, "This is my beloved Son, hear ye Him."

What a testimony! His friends and His enemies tell of His greatness. Heaven and earth sing His praises. God and man testify that He is wonderful.

III. Now What Do You Think of Christ?

1. *Do you think enough of Him to leave your sin and accept Him as your Saviour?* Many have done this in sincerity and no one has ever been disappointed in Him. He said, "Him that cometh to me I will in no wise cast out" (John 6:37). This literally means, "By no means will I thrust him out of the door." Here is the figure. A poor man in great distress comes to a rich nobleman's door. The rich man, in grace and mercy, opens his door, takes the poor man in and gives him all he needs. That's what Jesus does. No, He does more. His door is always open, His arms always extended in blessing and forgiveness. His "no wise cast out" equals to an affirmative, "I will kindly and graciously receive him."

Do you think enough of Jesus to give up your sin and come to Him? Or will you reject His loving invitation, hold on to your sin and go to hell?

2. *Do you think enough of Him to give Him first place in your life?* You must give Him some place. Where will you put Him? There is only one rightful place for Him and that is first place. No business, no pleasure, no comfort, no person should come before Jesus in your life.

When King George III was crowned as king of Great Britain, all the peers of the Empire came to the coronation and were allowed to wear their crowns as they were assembled before the throne. Then when the King mounted the throne, all of the peers came forward. They laid their crowns at the King's feet and kissed his scepter, thus signifying that they were submitting to his sovereignty over them.

As Christians we have a royal position under Christ. It is our privilege to lay all that we have and are at His feet. He must be Lord of lords and King of kings to us. Do you think enough of Him to put Him first in your life?

3. *Do you think enough of Him to tell others about Him?* He saved you — He snatched you as a brand from the burning. But there are others all around you who do not know

Him. Do you think enough of Him to tell them about His saving grace?

In the city of Boston years ago there was a faithful deacon. He said, "I cannot speak or pray in public. I can do very little for Christ. But I will set two extra plates at my table every Sunday and invite two people who are away from home to come to dinner. Then I can talk to them about Jesus." He did this for thirty years and won hundreds of lonely strangers to Jesus Christ. When he died 150 of these people came to his funeral. You don't have to be great to witness for Christ. You need only to love Him and love lost souls.

A pitcher went to the spring one day to be filled. "I hope," said the pitcher to the spring, "that I don't come too often to be filled." And the spring said, "You are just one of many who come." "Well, you are very generous," said the pitcher. "Do you give to all as you do to me?" And the spring replied, "I never refuse anyone. I just keep on flowing and there is always plenty for all those who come to me."

Now that's a picture of Jesus. He says, "Come to Me, all you who labor and are heavy laden. I have never turned anyone away and I won't turn you away. I have plenty of grace and salvation for all who come."

The following poem is the experience of many of us.

> You ask me how I gave my heart to Christ,
>   I do not know.
> There came a yearning in my soul for Him
>   So long ago.
> I found earth's flowers would fade and die,
>   I wept for something that could satisfy.
>
> And then, and then somehow
>   I seemed to dare
> To lift my broken heart to Him in prayer.
> I do not know, I cannot tell you how,
>   I only know He is my Saviour now.

Some years ago 1 conducted a revival in a Southern city. On Thursday night of the first week a young man came up to me at the close of the service. He told me that he wanted to talk to me in private. I saw the tears in his eyes, and felt that the Spirit of God was dealing with him. We went over to one of the Sunday school rooms and as soon as we entered the room he fell upon his knees and began to sob. I talked to him a few minutes and he was soon rejoicing in Christ. The next Thursday night he said to me, "I am twenty-four years of age. I have had a very happy life. But I want you to know that in this one week that I have been a Christian, I have had more happiness packed into my life than in all the twenty-four years that I have lived!"

That's what Jesus can do for anyone who comes to Him. "What think ye of Christ?"

9

THE LORD WANTS YOU

Luke 5:27-29

During World War II I saw a unique poster in front of an army recruiting office. In the center of the poster there was a cut-out round place with a mirror behind it. Underneath were the words, "Your country needs you." So, as a man read these words and looked into the mirror the poster became a personal message to him. He saw himself in the mirror and received the message that his country needed him. And this station enlisted more recruits than any station in the area.

But almost two thousand years ago a greater leader than Uncle Sam came into the world. He came to wage a greater war, to launch a greater program. He needed men to serve with Him so He went right down where men worked and lived, and there He gave His call, "Follow Me." And many men laid aside everything else and followed Him, some even to the death.

In the text we see Him going into a tax-collector's office to see a man named Levi. Now the Romans had levied a heavy tax on the people and it was Levi's task to collect these exorbitant taxes. For this reason he was despised of his fellow-countrymen. But the great leader, Jesus Christ, saw something in Levi that his neighbors could not see. Jesus saw a great heart hunger and He also saw a potential for great usefulness in Levi. So Jesus simply said, "Follow me." And we read that Levi "left all, rose up, and followed him."

His name was changed to Matthew. He wrote the first book in the New Testament, and followed Christ unto death.

The Lord needed Levi. He wanted him, so He called him and Levi followed Him. The same great leader stands even today before the hearts of men. He needs them — He wants them — He calls them. If you are out of the Kingdom, He calls you. If you are out of service, He calls you. If you are backslidden, He calls you to come back to Him, to find joy and happiness in His service. I hold the Gospel mirror of truth before you today and say to you, "Your Lord wants you. The great Saviour who died for you wants you and calls you to enlist in His service."

I. The Lord Wants You As a Star in His Crown

He wants you to be saved, to become one of His jewels, to have your name written down in "the Lamb's Book of Life." This is the purpose for which He came into the world. He looked down from the starry heights of heaven and saw you, a poor, lost, helpless sinner, doomed to eternal death. His heart went out to you; He wanted to save you. So He rushed down the long, hard, humiliating road that led to Calvary and there He gave His life away for you.

Out on the western prairies there is often no rainfall for months. Then is when the prairie catches on fire. The fires are often so great and the winds so strong that the flames shoot up twenty feet in the air, destroying everything. Men cannot escape these fires by running so what do they do? They light the grass all around them and then they stand in the center of the burned-over section. The flames roar toward them but they are not afraid, for the danger has already passed. And so the fires of hell and judgment burn toward us. Is there a place of safety for us? Yes, thank God, there is. There is one spot where the fires have already burned out. That place is Calvary. It was there that Christ bore all of our sin and guilt. If we'll just go to that spot we'll be forever safe. That's why Jesus came into the world, to take in His own body the fires of hell and judgment and to save us from them.

Now the greatest joy of His heart comes when a soul is saved. "Joy shall be in heaven over one sinner that repenteth" (Luke 15:7). This joy is the joy which comes to Jesus when a sinner is saved. Here is a young couple living in a sweet little home. They love each other, and are very happy. But their happiness is not complete. Then one day God gives them a precious little baby and life becomes sweeter and richer for them. The wife has a look on her face which she has never had before. The father rushes home from work to look with joy into the face of this tiny human being who has come to dwell with them. They rejoice that a child has been born. But their joy is nothing to compare with the joy that comes to Jesus when one for whom He died is born again.

The greatest desire of Christ is to have you as one of His children. In Revelation 3:20 He says, "Behold, I stand at the door, and knock: if any man hear my voice, and open the door, I will come in to him, and will sup with him, and he with me." He wants you as His child. Will you come to Him? "As many as received him, to them gave he power to become the sons of God, even to them that believe on his name" (John 1:12). He will receive you; He wants you.

II. THE LORD WANTS YOU TO BRING OTHERS TO HIM

The first desire of a new Christian is to bring someone else to Christ. He has tasted of the Lord and found Him so good, so sweet, that He wants others to know about Him. For sixteen years I prayed for and witnessed to one of my brothers. He sometimes rebuked me and told me that if he ever became a Christian, he wouldn't bother anyone else by talking to them about their salvation. And then it happened — he was saved in a revival where I preached. And, believe it or not, before the week was over he had won a fifty-five-year-old man to Christ in the shop where they worked and this man came to church and made his public profession of faith. Yes, when you feel Jesus in your heart you want someone else to know Him, also.

A telegraph messenger brought a telegram to a business man. After the man had read the telegram, he said to the messenger, "You have brought me a message, now I want to give you one." So he opened his Bible to the gospel of John and gave the boy the sweetest message ever delivered, the message which tells of a Saviour who died to save us from our sin. He soon won the boy to Christ. The man had something wonderful in his heart and he wanted to share it with someone else.

A university student once talked to his mother about his ambitions. He wanted to be a great lawyer, and wanted to become rich and famous. Just before he left home to return to the university for his senior year, his mother slipped a note in one of his pockets. Later, in his dormitory room, he opened the note and read it. It said, "For what shall it profit a man, if he gain the whole world, and lose his own soul?" (Mark 8:36). The truth of this text pierced his heart and soon he was converted.

The Lord wants to use us to bring others to Him. Years ago a young man named Paul Redfern flew on a solo flight to South America. He was last heard of when he was over the Caribbean. For many months search planes flew over the jungles and searching parties on foot sought for the young man, but he was never found. Why go to so much trouble? What was one aviator among so many? Why, he was everything to a mother, a father, his wife. Is it right to search for many days for a lost aviator and not to search for lost souls?

On the day of Pentecost Peter preached to a great crowd. On that day 3,000 people trusted Christ and joined the church. Did one sermon do it all? No. When Peter preached 119 other Christians witnessed for Christ. If any church could have ten or twenty or fifty members faithfully witnessing for Christ every week, scores would be saved every time the pastor preached.

General William Booth one day heard an infidel speak in a London park. This unbeliever said, "If I were a Christian and believed in heaven and hell, I would not stop night and day until I had warned men and sought to win them." This statement inspired Booth to establish the Salvation Army, whose original purpose was to win men to Christ. There is a heaven and a hell and men are lost without Christ. He wants to use us to win them.

The greatest joy on earth comes to a Christian when he is used to win someone to Christ. Years ago in Louisville, Kentucky, a good Christian woman said to a boy, "Would you like to go to Sunday school?" "Yes," he answered. He began to attend church and Sunday school every Sunday. One day the lady said, "Would you like to be a Christian?" And the boy again answered, "Yes." Sometime later she said, "Would you like to go to school and prepare to serve God?" And again the answer was "Yes." In due time this young man became a missionary to Japan. He was instrumental in leading Kagawa to Christ, and Kagawa was credited in winning thousands of his people to the Lord.

A godly salesman one day called upon the owner of a certain store. After a good order had been given to the salesman, he said to the store owner, "I am going to put your name on my prayer list." The owner was deeply moved by this gesture and the next time the salesman called on him, he took Christ as his Saviour. Then he won another man to Christ and that man won John R. Mott, who became one of the greatest Christians of the world, winning many souls to Christ. Let me ask you a question, "Are you doing anything to win anyone to Christ?"

III. THE LORD WANTS YOU AS A BUILDER OF HIS CHURCH

1. *The church is civilization's greatest asset.* Can you name any organization or institution which has meant as

much to the world as the church of Jesus Christ? Take the church and its influence out of the world and you would have only a jungle left.

Isn't it wonderful how the church has stood for nearly 2,000 years? A preacher comes to a small church. He stays there for ten or twenty or thirty years. He always has someone to listen to him as he preaches the Gospel. He has little help in the church. It is almost a one-man concern. Yet it goes on and on, doing the work of Christ. But look at some of the theaters. They have large staffs, spend thousands for publicity, change their programs every few days. Yet many of them fail. But the church stands because it is a divine institution and Jesus said that the gates of hell would not prevail against it.

The Russian "reds" said to a Christian many years ago, "We are going to pull down the churches. We'll topple every steeple and everything that will bring to men any idea of God." "All right," said the Christian, "but you'll have to pull down the stars also." But when the stars shine no more, the church will be living, triumphant in the heavens. Why? Because its foundation is the Lord Jesus Christ Himself.

2. *The church is a great blessing to the individual.* Did you ever stop to think of what the church has meant to your life. You came there as a child. There you were taught the good ways of life, and there you found Christ. There you were baptized, and there you found your staunchest friends. There is where you found comfort in time of sorrow, and found strength for the battles of life. What if you gave up the church? A void would be left that nothing else could fill. What a privilege to sit in a quiet church and worship God and listen to the message of God's man in the pulpit!

3. *We owe the church our loyalty and love.* Some years ago I met a man in the city who had been brought up in the small town where I was reared. I asked him what work he was doing. He said, "My job is to be the superintendent of the Sunday school in my church, but I work at City Hall to pay my expenses." He moved to another city and it was

several years before I saw him again. I asked him if he was still active in his church. He confessed that he was not. Then I reminded him of what he had once said to me and the tears came in his eyes. He said, "Yes, those were the happiest days of my life." There are hundreds of people like that. They are not happy, because they have given up the best life.

There are some church members who take some position of responsibility in the church and carry out their service to God for a time, then give it up. They ought to say, "My Lord and my church come first. I will give them my best. I'll let nothing come between me and my love obligations to my God."

4. *We owe the church our financial support.* God gives us the power to earn money, but He tells us that part of it must be given back to Him for the spread of the Gospel. And the part He requires is the tithe and, when possible, an offering over and above the tithe. The Bible tells us that we rob God when we withhold His tithe. We also rob ourselves of peace, a clear conscience in God's sight and the many blessings promised to the tither.

A missionary in the New Hebrides watched some natives killing hogs. These natives cut off the hogs' tails and put them over in a pile. When the missionary asked the natives why they did this, they replied, "The meat is for ourselves, the tails are for our gods." Some Christians are just as foolish and sinful. They take everything for themselves and give God the leftovers, if any. This is not right. It is sinful, wicked, disobedience toward God, robbing God.

A deacon asked one of the church members for a gift to the church. The man said, "The church is always wanting something." The deacon said, "I once had a precious son. He was very costly. I had to buy him clothes, shoes, books, many other things. But one sad night he died. Now he doesn't cost me a cent." As long as the church lives, as long as it stands to bless the world, it will cost something to operate. When it dies it won't need your help. But at the same time it won't be of any help to you. Thank God, the church lives and you and I have the privilege of helping to keep it going.

5. *We owe the church our service.* A few years ago there was a congressman named Buchanan. He became quite ill and the doctor said to him, "If you keep up your activitties you'll live about sixty days; if you retire you'll probably live several years. "I'll take the sixty days," he said, "I don't want to live uselessly." And he died in a few months' time. Surely none of us wants to live useless lives. If our hearts are right with God we would rather wear out than rust out.

IV. The Lord Wants You As a Living Witness of His Grace

I mean that He wants you to live in such a way that others can see Jesus in you.

> Let others see Jesus in you,
> Let others see Jesus in you.
> Keep telling the story, be faithful, be true,
> Let others see Jesus in you.

In a certain college there was a young Jewess who, because of her background, was prejudiced against Christianity. One day a very zealous Christian girl rushed into her room and tried to win her to Christ in a few minutes. Her efforts were met with failure. But this young Jewess had a wonderful sweet girl for a room-mate. She did not try to press the Jewish girl into a decision, but lived such a beautiful Christian life that the Jewess came one day to say, "I want what you have. Tell me how I can become a Christian." Yes, more than all else the world needs to see Jesus in you.

A little girl prayed, "Lord, I can't hold very much, but please fill me to overflowing. I can overflow lots." May God help us to be so filled with Christ that we will overflow and influence everyone around us. It doesn't matter how we die, but it matters supremely as to how we live.

Mrs. J. M. Dawson was the wife of the pastor of the First Baptist Church of Waco, Texas. She was the greatest woman speaker I have ever heard. In her Sunday school class there was a young woman who had two outstanding talents. She had a marvelous singing voice and she had the gift of healing in her hands. She was always wanting to bind up the wounds of little children. One day she burst into Mrs. Dawson's home and said, "I'm going to be a grand opera singer. My father is sending me away to study. Someday my name will be up in bright lights on Broadway. I'm going to be a star." Mrs. Dawson wished her well and sent her on her way.

Several years went by and Mrs. Dawson was speaking in a church in a southern city. This young lady was in the service and came up to speak to her. "What are you doing now?" Mrs. Dawson asked her. "I am head of a hospital for crippled children," the young woman replied. "How did it happen?" Mrs. Dawson asked, "What about your music?" She said, "One day I went to the missionary society to sing. After my song a woman spoke. She had been on the foreign field for thirty years. Her hair was gray and the lines of suffering showed on her face. She spoke of her work and I said to myself, 'Surely she can retire now; she won't go back over there.' But soon she said, 'I must go back and live for these for whom Christ died.' When I heard that I thought of my puny selfish efforts. God spoke to me that day, so I went back to school, took a nursing course and am now running this crippled children's hospital."

That afternoon Mrs. Dawson went out to the hospital and the young woman showed her through the various wards. Some of the children were in such pitiful condition that Mrs. Dawson's eyes filled with tears. "Doesn't it break your heart?" she asked, and the young woman replied, "But they are getting well." Then she went over to one bed and picked up a little negro boy and held him close to her heart while she sang, "Swing low, sweet chariot." Then she put the little boy back in his bed and said, "I'd rather have the privilege of holding that little black fellow in my arms and singing to him and helping to heal these little bodies than to be the greatest prima donna in grand opera."

She had found the true meaning of life, to love God and to serve others. Oh, that you and I might find it. The Lord wants you. He wants you in the greatest work in the world. "Who then will consecrate himself this day unto the Lord?"

10

GOD'S DANGER SIGNAL

Amos 4:12

Many of us are old enough to remember 7 December 1941. On the morning of that day scores of Japanese fighter and bomber planes attacked our fleet in Pearl Harbor, Honolulu. Many of our ships and planes were destroyed, thousands of our finest young men were killed, and fear gripped the hearts of every true American. President Roosevelt called it "a day that would live in infamy."

We were totally unprepared for that day. The attack was sudden and unexpected and deadly. If a merciful God had not intervened the Japanese would have come on to attack our West Coast and finally to subdue our country. Since that time we have tried to be prepared for another such emergency.

The wise man is always prepared. He prepares for sickness and accidents. He prepares for trouble and rainy days. He prepares for the welfare of his family. He prepares for his retirement years. The Boy Scouts have as their motto the simple words, "Be Prepared." God also believes in preparedness, so He thunders out from heaven, "Prepare to meet thy God. Get ready for the appointed hour of judgment.

However, many people who prepare for all of the exigencies of life do not heed God's warning. They prepare for everything else except for that sure and ultimate confrontation with Almighty God. They are too busy with the affairs of this life to make any preparation for meeting God.

The Christian must meet God as surely as the sinner. The Christian is to face the Lord at the "judgment seat of Christ" (Rom. 14:10). There his works shall be judged and he shall be rewarded according to those works. What a pity it is that so many Christians are doing nothing for Christ. They will be saved "as if by fire," but there'll be no reward for them when they stand before the Saviour who died for them. The unsaved man must meet God at the judgment of "The Great White Throne" (Rev. 20:11). There his works as a sinner will be judged and his future punishment set. Then he will go into the lake of fire. As there will be degrees of reward for the saved, so shall there be degrees of punishment for the unsaved.

In this message let us ponder three questions:

1. WHY PREPARE TO MEET GOD?
2. HOW PREPARE TO MEET GOD?
3. WHEN PREPARE TO MEET GOD?

1. WHY PREPARE TO MEET GOD?

1. *Because God demands it.* Like a river running through a valley, like an unbroken thread there runs all the way through the Bible God's command for us to prepare to meet Him. It is tragic not to obey that command.

We often hear someone say, "I have broken one of the Ten Commandments." The truth is that we break ourselves upon these commandments. But why should anyone break himself upon this commandment? Why should he go through life and come to the end of the way unprepared?

A slave was mourning over the death of his master. Someone asked him if he thought his master had gone to heaven. He said, "I guess not, because he always made some preparation when he was going somewhere. If he was going to the city or to the springs or to the mountains, he always spent several days getting ready. I never did hear of his making any preparation for going to heaven, so I guess he hasn't gone there." But this is one of God's commands and the wise man obeys it.

2. *Because of our sinful condition.* God is holy and righteous; we are sinful and unrighteous. We are not ready, in our natural state, to meet a pure and holy God. As long as we walk in sin we can never walk with a holy God. Only Christ can give us that holiness and righteousness that will enable us to face God.

3. *Because of our lost condition.* "The Son of man is come to seek and to save that which was lost" (Luke 19:10). Oh, I wish we could see all the tragedy wrapped up in that word "lost." When the Lindbergh baby was lost all the world became concerned. We listened to every radio broadcast, we read every news item in order to learn something about a baby that was lost. But there is something worse than that. That baby died and was taken to the Father's house above. But souls are lost, lost without God and without hope, lost for time and eternity. That's why we should try to win souls in order that the lost might be found and saved.

When a man loses his business, that is not the greatest loss. When a man loses his health, that is not the greatest loss. When a man loses his sight, even that is not the greatest loss. But when a man loses his soul that is the greatest loss of all.

Being lost means eternal separation from God. Jesus said, "I go to prepare a place for you . . . that where I am, there ye may be also" (John 14:2, 3). But unless we prepare to meet God we'll not be with Christ in that place He has prepared. We'll be cut off from Him forever. Lost men will be cut off from every blessing, from friends and loved ones. But worse of all, they will be cut off from God forever.

This loss means eternal suffering. Jesus said, "Except ye repent, ye shall all likewise perish" (Luke 13:3). He tells us that the rich man who went to hell cried out, "I am tormented in this flame" (Luke 16:24). In Revelation 20:15 we are told that the lost will be cast into the "lake of fire," there to be tormented day and night forever.

Do you think you can go on without Christ and that at the end of the way it will be well with you forever? No. The Bible tells us that conscious suffering awaits every lost person. The soul of man lives on. The saved are in heaven, the lost in hell. If death ends it all, life isn't worth the struggle. But there is another life and those who are not ready to meet God are to spend that life in endless shame and suffering.

II. How Prepare to Meet God?

1. *We must leave our sin.* This is what the Bible calls "repentance." This is an act in which we turn away from sin and turn toward God. It is coming over to God and taking His side against sin.

A boy reached down into a jar, but he couldn't get his hand out because he had doubled his hand up into a fist. Someone told him to release his fingers, but he said, "I can't do it. I have a dime in my hand." And so men who hold on to their sin can never reach God. But Jesus comes and says, "Put it all on me, I'll save you. I'll wash away all your sin; I'll make you ready to meet God."

There are two things you can do about your sin. You can hold on to it and be lost forever. Or you can turn from it to Christ and be saved forever.

2. *We must come to Christ.* Not only are we to leave our sin, but we must go farther — we must turn in faith to Christ. It is "repentance toward God, and faith toward our Lord Jesus Christ" (Acts 20:21). Our repentance is toward God, for it is His commandments that we have disobeyed. It is faith toward Jesus Christ, for He is the object of saving faith.

A boy was leaving for the war. His mother gave him a Bible, and urged him to read it and follow its teachings. But he neglected to follow his mother's advice. Then there came the day when he was facing a fierce battle. He trembled like a leaf and became as pale as death. "Are you afraid to die?"

an older soldier asked him. "No," he replied, "but I am afraid of what comes after death." If he had followed the directions in his Bible he would have had no need to fear death or what follows after.

But the very hour a man says, "I will leave my sin and trust Christ, the great Sin-bearer," in that moment he will be saved. God says, "Come now, and let us reason together, saith the Lord: though your sins be as scarlet, they shall be as white as snow; though they be red like crimson, they shall be as wool" (Isa. 1:18). A great loving, merciful, reasonable God warns you to prepare to meet your Maker.

III. WHEN PREPARE TO MEET GOD?

Listen to three warnings from God's Word. "Now is the accepted time; behold, now is the day of salvation" (II Cor. 6:2). "Today if ye will hear his voice, harden not your hearts" (Heb. 4:7). "Boast not thyself of tomorrow; for thou knowest not what a day may bring forth" (Prov. 27:1).

Dr. L. R. Scarborough preached one Sunday morning in the First Baptist Church of Little Rock, Arkansas. When he gave the Gospel invitation a fine doctor came forward to give his heart to Christ. That afternoon the doctor was making some house calls on some of his patients. He drove up to one house, stopped his car, then slumped over on his steering wheel and was gone. What if he had not come to Christ that morning?

1. *Come to Christ now because delay makes it harder to make a decision.* We are told that there is a sign on the Niagara River some distance above the falls, which read, "Past Redemption Point." To go down the river beyond that point means that there is no redemption, no hope. You will be carried over the falls to death on the rocks below. We are all going down the river of life. There is a point beyond which, if we go, there is no hope, no redemption, for us. A man postpones his salvation time and time again. Each postponement makes a decision harder. One day there will

come a time when that man feels no impulse, no desire, to be saved. The Spirit ceases to strive with him. He has gone past the point of redemption.

If you place a bandage over one eye and keep it there indefinitely, you'll lose the sight of that eye. If you tie your arm to your side and leave it there indefinitely, you'll lose the use of that arm. And if you fail to exercise your choice of trusting Christ, it will become harder and harder until there comes a time when you cannot make a choice.

Dr. George W. Truett tells about riding from the funeral parlor to the cemetery after conducting the funeral of one of his members. In the car with him was a man who was not a Christian. The preacher pressed the claims of Christ upon the man as they rode along and the man said to him, "Years ago I was greatly moved and touched in a revival meeting. I felt that I would die if I did not yield my heart and life to Christ. But I postponed the matter until finally the feeling left me. Now I have no desire and feel no impulse toward making a decision for the Lord." Dr. Truett said that he remained with the man for quite a while and talked to him at length, but that the man insisted that he had "crossed over the line" and that there was no hope for him. Yes, it seems that a person can postpone this important matter until it is too late.

2. *Come to Christ now so that life here might be saved.* Life on this earth is never lived at its best unless it is lived for Christ. If you knew that you would be alive ten years from now and if you knew you could be saved then, I would still say to you, "Don't wait. Come to Christ now. Give those ten years to Christ and let Him give you the happiness and usefulness that He alone can give. Don't give those ten years to Satan and the world."

What about your influence? It can be a powerful thing, whether or not you are conscious of it. If you live for Satan your influence will hurt others. If you live for Christ your influence will help others.

A man who was sixty-eight years of age was gloriously

saved. He became a very faithful Christian and church member. One day he came to the pastor's study, weeping as if his heart was breaking. He said to the pastor, "I have been concerned about my married sons and their families. I go to see them and I try to get them to turn to Christ and the church and they laugh and say to me, 'Dad, when we are sixty-eight we'll do that.' I would gladly have my right arm cut off if I could recall the influence I had on them when they were young and when I was not a Christian."

A certain boy had a dream one night and woke up, crying. His father tried to comfort him and asked him to tell him about the dream. The boy hesitated to tell him but the father insisted. Finally the boy said, "Daddy, I dreamed that you had your hand on my throat and that you were choking me to death." But that is not a dream in some families. Because of the negative and sinful influence of fathers and mothers, they are sending their children to hell.

I am thinking now of a certain family. The father has a high position in the business and civic life of his city. The mother's interest is only in social and worldly affairs. They live in a lovely home. They have five beautiful children. But these parents never go to church, although they are church members. They never give a penny to the cause of Christ; they never take the children to Sunday school or to any spiritual activity. In other words, they live as if there were no God, no future life, no judgment. By the lives that they live they are influencing their children away from God and every Christian principle of life. The blood of the children's souls will be upon their hands at the judgment.

The greatest privilege of a woman is to hold a new-born babe in her arms. The greatest privilege of a man is to have a little boy or girl call him "daddy." You owe something to the children God has given you. You owe it to them to live for Christ and to set the right Christian example before them.

3. *Come to Christ now and be ready for the end of life.* We don't know when that time will come — the angels don't

know. It may be soon — it won't be long for any of us. It may be at night when all the world is quiet, when the Death Angel comes for you. It may be at dawn, when the world is waking. It may be at noon when the world is busy. It may be in the fall, when the leaves are turning into a myriad of colors. It may be in the winter, when the earth is white with snow. It may be at Christmas time when bells ring out their lovely anthems. It may be at the New Year, when the whistles are ushering in another year. The important thing is this — are you ready for that hour?

One day we must go out to meet the great Judge of all the universe, there to give an account of these little lives of ours. You can be ready, not because of your good life, your fine character, your good works, but because you have repented of your sin and have sincerely trusted Jesus Christ as your Lord and Saviour.

A young man went into a man's office and bought a life insurance policy from a Christian insurance salesman. On the day that the policy was delivered the insurance man said to the younger man, "You have taken out some life insurance to protect your family after you are gone, but what about some eternal life insurance that will cover you for time and eternity?" The young man was immediately interested. The insurance man talked to him about Christ and soon they knelt by the desk and the young man trusted Christ. He went out of the office in a happy mood, being well-insured for this life and the life to come.

On the way home the young man was run over by a truck and killed. What if he hadn't used his last chance to trust the Saviour. "Prepare to meet thy God." Are you prepared?

11

TWELVE HOURS TO LIVE

Luke 12:16-21

Jesus was the most effective preacher who ever lived. He knew how to grip the attention of His congregation, and how to make His sermons interesting. He filled His messages with down-to-earth illustrations. On one occasion He was talking about covetousness, about those who thought more of the world than about the things of God. He was saying that it was not what men had, but what they were, that counted.

So he used a striking illustration. He said that one year a well-to-do farmer had a very fine crop. In fact the crop was so bountiful that he didn't have storage space enough for it. So he said to himself, "I will pull down my barns and build bigger barns in which to store my earthly goods." But about that time a voice within whispered to him. His soul said, "What are you going to do about your spiritual life, about your relationship to God?" And the man answered, "Oh, soul, don't worry about that. I'll attend to spiritual matters later. In the meantime eat, drink and be merry." Then God spoke. Notice what He called the man. "Thou fool," God said, "this night you're going to die and leave all these worldly things behind."

Then Jesus made the application. "So is everyone," he said, "who thinks only of things down here and leaves God out." But the tragedy is that so many people are doing this today. They are not necessarily rich — they may never be rich. Yet they are giving all of their time and energy and attention to this world and forgetting God.

Well, this man had just about twelve hours to live. Yet he spent those hours as he had lived, grasping the things of the world and not looking up to God. He thought of gold instead of God, of pleasure instead of people, of ease instead of eternity. Suppose that you knew you had just twelve hours to live, what would you do? I am afraid some of us would have to make some radical changes.

Some years ago, on a Sunday night, Orson Welles broadcast a very vivid description of the invasion of the world by men from Mars. Of course, it was all simple fantasy. But a certain deacon was at home listening to the radio when he should have been at church. Not knowing that the broadcast was just a dramatic presentation by a great actor, he was frightened almost out of his wits. So he ran to a place of refuge, his church. He rushed into the auditorium, stopped the preacher in the middle of the sermon and told the people that the world was coming to an end and that they should prepare for judgment. He changed his way of life in a few minutes when he thought death was near.

Now if you knew that you had only twelve hours to live, what would you do? Let me tell you several things I believe you and I would want to do.

I. We Would Want to Be Sure of Our Salvation

Are you sure that you have been really and truly saved? Are you certain that you are a child of God? Do you know that you have had a saving experience with Christ? Paul could say, "I know whom I have believed, and am persuaded that he is able to keep that which I have committed unto him against that day" (II Tim. 1:12). He was not trusting in his church membership, his baptism, his preaching, his good works, but he put his trust in the One who said, "I am the way, the truth, and the life: no man cometh unto the

Father, but by me" (John 14:6). If we had to trust in our own goodness or our own works we would be on the road to hell. But putting all our trust in Him we can say: "My hope is built on nothing less than Jesus' blood and righteousness."

Are you sure you are saved? Certainly even many of our church people don't live like it. If they would only judge themselves by their fruit they would have reason to doubt their salvation. What are the conditions of salvation? "Verily, verily, I say unto you, He that heareth my word, and believeth on him that sent me, hath everlasting life, and shall not come into condemnation; but is passed from death unto life" (John 5:24).

We are told here that if a man hears the Gospel, turns from his sin and trusts Christ, he will have everlasting life. He will not come into condemnation but has passed from death unto life. And surely such an experience will bring about a change in that man's life. He'll know that he is saved and he'll live like it.

You don't go to hell because you fail to live the Christian life and carry out your Christian duties. You fail to do these things because you have never met Christ and therefore you are on the road to hell.

I read of a great preacher of other days who lay awake one night, saying to himself, "I wonder if I am really saved." Then in a minute he got out of bed, knelt down and prayed." "Oh, Lord Jesus, if I have never trusted Thee I do now with all my heart."

The only thing that will matter when you get to the end of your way is your salvation. It won't matter how much you've made or where you have lived or how many friends you have. The only thing that will matter is your relationship to Christ. If you knew you were going to die tonight you would want to be sure of your salvation. Well, you may die tonight, so why not make sure of your salvation right now.

II. We Would Want to Be Affiliated With a New Testament Church

If we had only twelve hours to live we would want to be an active and faithful member of a New Testament church. Some people come to Christ in one place — they become members of a church in that place, then they move to some other place and live out of the church for years. When you ask them if they have been saved they say, "I hope so." They are really telling the truth. They have gotten so far away from God that they have lost the assurance of their salvation.

I believe that you can't keep a person out of a church fellowship if he has been really and truly saved. They will know that Christ saved them to serve in and through His church and they'll get in one as quickly as possible when they move from one place to another.

Do you want your life as a Christian to count for Christ? Then you should plant your life in a New Testament church. How can you know which church is a New Testament church? Just read your New Testament and see what the churches back there believed and practiced. Then find the church that believes and practices the same thing and join it. Approach the subject with an open mind, and ask for the guidance of the Holy Spirit. He will direct you.

But someone says, "There are so many hypocrites in the church." This is true, but you'll also find the best people there. You don't let hypocrites keep you away from anything else. There are some doctors who are hypocrites, but that doesn't keep you from calling on the good ones when you are sick. There are some bankers who are hypocrites, but that doesn't keep you from using the service of a good bank. There are some teachers who are hypocrites, but you don't keep your children away from school because of that. Angel Martinez said that he bought a dozen eggs and two of them were hypocrites. They were not what they ought to have been. But that doesn't keep us from eating eggs.

The great preacher, Charles Haddon Spurgeon, had an apple orchard. One day he looked out of the window and saw his neighbor slipping into the orchard and stealing several apples. He sampled one or two apples, made a bitter face and threw them away. Giving up in disgust he went home. Then Spurgeon went out into the orchard, filled a basket with apples and carried them over to the neighbor. The man was embarrassed. He confessed that he had already sampled the apples and found them too bitter to eat. "Yes," said Spurgeon, "I planted some sour crabapple trees there at the entrance to the orchard to scare off anyone who wanted to steal them. But I planted the best trees in the center of the orchard and this basket is filled with the sweet apples from these trees."

In like manner we can find some sour crabapple hypocrites around the edge of the church, but you'll also find some sweet and wonderful Christians in the center of it. In the Bible there is the story of tares and wheat growing in the same field. And Jesus said, "Let them alone until harvest time. Don't tear up the whole field now. The tares and wheat will be separated at harvest time." So we are not to shun the church because there are some hypocrites in it. They'll be taken care of at harvest time.

For nearly two thousand years the good and the bad have been in the church. But in spite of the bad, the hypocrites, the church marches on. One of Jesus' disciples, the treasurer, was dishonest. He betrayed the Saviour. The chief disciple denied Jesus with an oath. But the church swept on to victory. And everything good in our society today has come about because of the influence of the church.

So if you knew you were going to die within twelve hours, you would certainly want to be a member of a New Testament church. You may die tonight, so if you are a Christian you ought to line up with a church where you live and where you can serve.

III. We Would Want to Make Restitution for Our Wrongs

If we had only twelve hours to live I am sure we could think of some restitution which we should make.

If a man really wants to get right with God he must make things right with others. One day Zacchaeus, a publican and a sinner, met Jesus. This experience completely transformed his life. How do we know that? Listen to him, "If I have taken anything wrongfully from any man I will restore it fourfold." He was just beginning to live, up to that time he had simply been existing. If you are not right with your fellowman you are not really living.

Would you like to go out into eternity twelve hours from now, knowing that you had cheated someone? That you had put over a fast deal on someone? That you had hurt someone with your gossip? No, you would be as busy as could be trying to straighten out these matters before going out to meet God.

Is there even the least thing between you and anyone in the world? Then let me urge you to make matters right now. Keep your heart clean, so that if you died tonight it would be well with you.

IV. We Would Want to Get Right on the Money Question

Now you are saying, "Wait a minute, preacher, with only twelve hours to live, this isn't any time to think about money, is it?" Yes, it is very important that we always be right on the money question.

First, we ought not to leave any debts when we go. If there are some debts we ought to arrange in some way for them to be paid off immediately. The world often judges our Christianity by the way we pay our debts. If you do not pay your debts you are not honest. And the world has no respect for a dishonest man's profession of religion. Every

Christian ought to make a will; he ought to provide for his obligations to be cared for.

But here is something more important. It is the matter of your tithe, the money you owe God — His tithe. The tithe is not yours to spend; it belongs to God. The tithe ought to be paid as the income is made. The top tenth, the first tenth, is always to be paid to God. I did not say "given to God." The tithe is a debt that you owe Him. Pay that first, then anything above that is a gift to Him.

A preacher went into a hospital room to see an elderly man who was recuperating from a very serious operation and heard that man angrily arguing with his doctor. The doctor explained to the preacher that the old man owed a small sum to a local merchant. He was trying to get the old man to sign a check in payment of this small sum. But the old man thought the doctor was trying to trick him out of his life's savings. The doctor asked the preacher to intercede. The preacher looked at the check, saw that everything was all right and persuaded the old man to sign.

Do you get the point? A few days before the old man had been near death and he was glad to trust his life in the hands of the doctor. But now he was not willing to trust him with a check for a few dollars. There are many Christians like the old man. When they were lost and on the way to hell they were willing to turn their soul's eternal welfare over to Jesus Christ and trust Him to save them. But now they are not willing to trust Him with the tithe which He asks of them.

You know God is going to be fair. You know He will keep His promise. You know He blesses the tither. The one who can save you and take you to heaven can surely take care of you in this world.

In one of our churches a certain man would come by the church on a week-day once a month and leave his tithe. But he came to church every Sunday and one of the secretaries asked him why he didn't wait until Sunday and then put his offering in the plate. He replied, "I have a serious heart condition and I could go at any minute. So when I get my pension check I go to the bank and cash it, then I bring God's tithe to the church. I don't want to have any of God's money in my pocket when I go."

That's the way it should be with every Christian. If you had only twelve hours to live you would want to get right on the money question.

V. WE WOULD WANT TO WITNESS TO SOMEONE ABOUT JESUS CHRIST

You can think of someone right now who is lost. If you knew that you had only twelve hours to live you would surely want to hasten to them and try to win them to Christ.

In the early years of my ministry I knew a man who lay on his deathbed. He was a Christian and a faithful church member, but he had never been a strong witness for Christ. He ran a grocery store on the main street of a small town and was highly respected by the other businessmen in town. Knowing that he was soon to die he called these men to his bedside, one by one, and pled with them to give their hearts and lives to Christ. His testimony during those last hours was more effective than all the sermons preached in that town that year.

Do you expect to meet anyone in heaven who is there because of your efforts? If you are faithful in your living and in your giving perhaps someone will meet you on the streets of glory and thank you for what you did to bring the Gospel to him. It may be someone you've never seen or heard of. Sometime ago I received a letter from a woman in Tampa, Florida. She wrote, "I was not a Christian, but my mother-in-law gave me your book on Christ's Second Coming. I read the book, saw my lost condition and gave my heart to Christ. I have been baptized and have joined the church. I am leaving now to join my husband who is stationed in Japan. He will be so happy now to have a

Christian wife." That's the thing that counts. Are you doing anything to win anyone to Christ?

Well, if you knew you had only twelve hours to live, surely you would want to straighten everything out and do the best you could for Christ and others. Do you know that you have more than twelve hours to live? Can any doctor on earth guarantee that you are going to live even one more hour?

Sixty-five people boarded a plane in Chicago for a flight to New York. They were laughing and talking and joking. The plane crashed just outside of New York and everyone on board was killed. Did they know that they were going to die when they boarded that plane? We read each year of several hundred people who are killed on the highway during the Christmas holidays. When they left home, looking forward to the trip and to a reunion with their loved ones, they did not know that this would be their last trip. A few days ago thirty-eight miners perished in the bosom of the earth. When they went down the mine shaft in the elevator they were teasing each other, laughing and joking. They didn't know that would be the last elevator ride they would ever take. I knew a woman who slumped over and died as she finished eating her breakfast. When she sat down at the table she didn't know this would be the last meal she would ever eat.

You sit in your comfortable pew in your church on Sunday morning. You don't know whether you'll ever sit there again. So now is the time to get everything right with God and man so you'll be ready to go when the summons comes from on high.

Now, after you get ready you can wait in peace as Paul did. See him yonder in that cell. He knows he is to die the next day. The ax is sharp, the executioner ready to swing it. What does the great man of God say? "I am now ready to be offered and the time of my departure is at hand." The word "departure" carries the meaning of a ship leaving the dock, a ship that will soon sail into some other port. So it was with Paul, so it can be with us. We simply sail out from this old earth to land in the port of eternal joy. So let us give our hearts to Christ, let us live at our best for Him every minute. Then if we go out within twelve hours we can say, "Lord, I am ready. I am glad that I can come home to be with Thee forever."

But you may say, "It's all right for you to talk that way to someone who is approaching death, but I expect to live many more years." Well, what better way to live than in trusting Christ, in serving Him and His church, in laying up treasures in heaven? You are never ready to die unless you are living rightly for God.

One day a tired preacher decided to take a horseback ride into the woods. As he entered the woods he dropped the reins and let the horse go wherever he wanted to go. Soon he came to a clearing. In the middle of the clearing there was a small cabin, with an old woman sitting out in front. Getting off his horse the preacher walked over and talked to the old woman. "Do you live here alone?" he asked. And she said, "Yes, sir, just Jesus and me. That's all, just Jesus and me." The preacher said that suddenly the small clearing seemed like a part of heaven and he could almost hear the angels singing.

Just Jesus and me, that's enough. Just Jesus and me, that abundantly satisfies. Just Jesus and me, against all the sorrows and troubles of this world. Just Jesus and me, against sin and Satan. Just Jesus and me, against death and the grave. Just Jesus and me, for all eternity. Is He yours today? Would you be ready to meet Him if you had only twelve hours to live?

12

SIX WATERPOTS FILLED WITH BLESSINGS

John 2:1-12

One day Jesus and His mother and the disciples received an invitation to a wedding. It must have read something like this: "Mr. and Mrs. Solomon Levy request your presence at the marriage of their daughter, Sylvia, to Mr. Jacob Ginsberg, on June 20th at 7 in the evening in the synagogue. You are also invited to the wedding supper which will follow in the home of the bride's parents, 220 Main Street, in Cana of Galilee."

I imagine that there were different reactions when the invitation was received. Mary may have said, "Sylvia is a beautiful girl and she'll make a lovely bride." Maybe Jesus said, "Yes, and she is marrying a fine young man. I have seen him often in the synagogue services." And the disciples said, "Yes, and Solomon sets a good table. The wedding supper will be a bountiful feast. Let's go." So they decided to go to the wedding and the wedding feast.

At the time appointed they were in the synagogue for the wedding. And after the solemn religious ceremony they went to the Levy home for the wedding feast. They ate and drank and laughed and rejoiced with the young couple. Then, in the middle of the feast, the wine gave out. With all that the Bible says about the evils of strong drink, I think we can be sure that this wine was not an intoxicating drink or Jesus would not have been drinking it. Well, Mary told Jesus of the predicament so He turned to the servants and gave them an order.

He told them to fill six waterpots with water and carry them in to the master of ceremonies. They did this and when the ruler of the feast dipped into the first waterpot, behold, he brought up not water, but the sweetest wine. He took a taste of the wine and said to the bridegroom, "You have certainly surprised us. Usually the best wine is served at the first and the sorry wine later. But this is wonderful wine. You have saved the best until the last." This was the first recorded miracle of Jesus, turning plain water into the sweetest wine.

But that's true of all that Jesus does. He takes all of life and turns its bitterness into sweetness. He causes all things to work together for good to them that love Him. So right now let us imagine that these six waterpots are before us. And let us put the experiences of life into them and see what Christ gives in return.

I. We Put Our Sins in the First Waterpot and He Gives Us Salvation in Return

He said to Nicodemus, "Ye must be born again." He was simply saying, "Put all of your sins on Me and I'll save you." He said in Matthew 11:28, "Come unto me, all ye that labour and are heavy laden, and I will give you rest." He was simply saying, "Put your sin on Me and I'll save you." He said in John 6:37, "Him that cometh to me I will in no wise cast out." He was simply saying, "Put you sin on Me and I'll save you." He said in John 3:18, "He that believeth on him [the Son] is not condemned." He was simply saying, "Put your sin on Me and there will be no condemnation for you. I will save you eternally."

Oh, how inclusive is His promise to save. "Whosoever will" is His promise. This includes everyone — the good and the bad, the rich and the poor, the high and the low. In one of our churches a young woman came forward and said to the pastor, "I want to become a Christian and join this church." The pastor rejoiced with her and told her to sit down on the front seat and fill out a membership card. As she sat there she began to weep and the pastor sat down beside her to help her. But she said, "I have made a mistake. I wrote my name on the card as Mrs. Brown, but I am not married. I wrote it that way because I have a baby in the nursery. But I made a mistake in trying to join your church. You don't want anyone like me, so I'll tear up the card and go back to my seat." But the kindhearted pastor assured her that she had not made a mistake and showed her from God's Word that Jesus was willing and happy to have her come to Him and be saved. The pastor baptized her and received her in to the church. Now, he says, she is a faithful Christian and church member and her little boy is being brought up under the ministry of that church.

Oh, how wonderful it is that we can bring our sins to Jesus and He will give us His marvelous salvation.

> There is a fountain filled with blood
> Drawn from Immanuel's veins,
> And sinners plunged beneath that flood
> Lose all their guilty stains:

> The dying thief rejoiced to see
> That fountain in his day,
> And there may I, though vile as he,
> Wash all my sins away.

In a recent national election some men wore a button which said, "I'm in the book." They meant that they had been registered to vote. But there is a more important book than the voter registration book. It is the Lamb's Book of Life. When we come to Jesus our names are written in that book. He takes our sins and gives us salvation.

> Is your name written there,
> On the page bright and fair,
> In the book of God's kingdom,
> Is your name written there?

Our church services in the First Baptist Church of El Paso were broadcast over radio, and later over television. A young high school senior listened to these broadcasts several weeks, then he began to attend our church services. One day he walked to the front and gave his heart to Jesus. Later on he felt that God was calling him to a lifetime of Christian service. He went ahead to college, to seminary and for postgraduate study. He is now Dr. James A. Brooks, professor of New Testament in the New Orleans Baptist Seminary. He came to Jesus with his sin and Jesus gave him His salvation.

At the same time there was a man over eighty years of age in the city, a multi-millionaire but an unsaved man. His wife was a devoted Christian and I often visited with her and prayed with her for the salvation of her husband. I was in another state when she died and this man sent a private plane for me, so that I could come home and conduct her funeral service. After that time I visited him several times and talked to him about his soul's salvation. Finally, one morning he came forward and confessed Christ as his personal Saviour. At that time he was eighty-three years of age. He died when he was eighty-six years of age and I conducted his funeral. He left millions of dollars behind, much of it for charitable purposes. Like the high school senior he brought his sins to Jesus and the Lord gave him His salvation. Over the years I have seen thousands of others who heard the Gospel, came to Christ with their sins, and received His salvation.

A good Christian woman was on a train, making a trip from the West coast to the East Coast, a trip of several days. One woman on the Pullman made it a point to talk to everyone about her religion of Christian Science, a religion which cuts under the atoning blood of Christ. This Christian woman felt conscience-stricken, because she knew Jesus in saving faith and was not witnessing to anyone. She decided that she would seek a good opportunity to tell someone about her Saviour. She noticed that one berth was not made up and she asked the porter about it. He told her that a young man who was quite ill was behind the drawn curtains. She sent word to him, asking if she might talk to him for a few minutes.

When she secured this permission she went to his berth and he drew back the curtains. She found herself looking at a young man whose face was flushed with tuberculosis. She chatted pleasantly with him for a while, brought him a magazine, then went back to her seat. Then she thought, "Maybe he needs to know about Christ and I didn't use the opportunity to witness to him." So she went back and said to him, "Young man, are you a Christian?" He replied, "No, I am not and I know I am going home to die. I was just wondering if there was anyone on this train who could tell me how to be saved." Then she poured out the story of Christ to him and told him how to be saved.

The next morning she looked back in on him and he said, "Isn't it wonderful? After you left me I began to think of what you said, of how merciful and forgiving Christ was, so I called upon Him to save me. And suddenly it seemed that He came down and bent over me and took all my sins and fears away. Now this morning I am happy in Him and I am not afraid of the future."

Oh, it happens, it really does! When we look to Him, when we come with our sins to the foot of the cross, He gives us salvation and peace and eternal life. And we ought to be busy every day, telling people about His saving grace as the woman did.

II. WE PUT OUR PRAYERS IN THE SECOND WATERPOT AND HE GIVES US THE ANSWERS

O, how sweet is the privilege of prayer! Over and over God says, "Call on Me, call on Me." He has all that we need and is ready to give it to us when we ask for it. He says, "Ask, and it shall be given you; seek, and ye shall find; knock, and it shall be opened unto you" (Matt. 7:7). Many things have been wrought by prayer! Lives have been changed, problems have been solved, troubled hearts have found peace because of prayer.

My brother, George, who has now gone on to glory, was converted under my preaching when he was thirty-eight years of age. He didn't have an advanced education. He didn't learn many theological terms, but he learned how to pray. He was sick for some time before he died, but he had a wonderful wife who looked after his every need. One night she went to his bedside and asked him if he was ready to go to sleep. He said, "I will be after I have talked to the Man upstairs." There was nothing irreverent about what he said. He just felt that close to God. Yes, sweet is the privilege of prayer.

Simon Peter, the chief apostle, was put in prison and was to be slain the next morning. That night a group of Christians gathered in John Mark's house and prayed for their preacher. "Oh, Lord," they prayed, "we just can't lose Peter. He is the chief apostle; he is the boldest of all. Please save Peter and bring him back to us." In the prison sixteen soldiers were guarding Peter and he was sleeping between two soldiers to whom he was chained. He was the only Christian asleep in the city that night, for the others were praying. God heard those prayers and sent an angel down to the prison. He awoke Peter, took off his chains without waking the soldiers, and led Peter out through the iron gates. Peter went straight to the house where his friends were praying.

When he knocked on the door the Christians were too busy praying to answer the door, so they sent a little girl named Rhoda to the door. She heard Peter's voice but was too excited to open the door. She ran back to tell the little group that Peter was at the door. They said, "You are crazy." But she kept on saying, "I am sure it was Peter," and they said, "he has been killed already and that's his ghost." But Peter kept on knocking, and when they finally opened the door, there stood Peter, grinning at them. They were astonished beyond measure. They had been praying all night, and when their prayers were answered it was just too wonderful to believe.

Why do you neglect your prayer life? How can you live without it? Don't you believe God's promises? Bring all your doubts and burdens and troubles to Him. Put all your prayers in the second waterpot and take out the glorious answers He will give you.

III. WE PUT OUR PROBLEMS IN THE THIRD WATERPOT AND HE GIVES US GUIDANCE

We are living in a complex age. There are many problems facing us today. Life is not a simple thing anymore. We need a wisdom far beyond our own. Well, God has that wisdom and is ready to share it with us. In James 1:5 we read, "If any of you lack wisdom, let him ask of God, that giveth to all men liberally, and upbraideth not; and it shall be given him." We lack wisdom, but we don't always seek for it in the right place. We don't go to God for it.

Much of our trouble comes because we run ahead of God. We say, "This is what I will do," without consulting God. Jesus often uses the term, "Mine hour is not yet come." He didn't rush into things; He waited on God. Then when the right time came He did the right thing.

I had a fine man in my church who was one of our ushers and a very fine Christian. He had a responsible position and flew a private plane to many appointments. One day he wanted to make a plane trip and he did the right thing first. He consulted the flight tower about flying conditions in the area. They told him that the weather was not suitable for flying. But he must have said, "I'll get along all right. I know how to handle this plane. I've flown in that area often, so I'll go ahead." He flew away and the winds caught him in the mountains and brought him down to his death. He did the right thing — he consulted the authority — but he did not take the advice he received. He thought his way was best. We are that way, also. We think our way is best and we plunge in only to meet calamity. The greatest sorrow I suffered during my ministerial career came when I ran ahead of God, following my own counsel instead of following the leading of the Holy Spirit.

When Hezekiah was king of Judah, Sennacherib and a great Assyrian army came up against him. Sennacherib sent a blasphemous letter to Hezekiah. He said, "We are coming to wipe out Jerusalem and all that are in it. We know you trust in God but we are not afraid of Him. We have gone against other nations which trusted in their gods and we have destroyed them, just as we will destroy you." Did Hezekiah call in his generals and have a council of war? Did he plan a new battle strategy? Did he say, "We had better surrender right now"? No, he did a simple thing, a very wise thing. He went to the house of God and spread the letter out so that the Lord could read it over his shoulder. Then he prayed and asked God to intervene and save the city. And God did just that. The angel of the Lord came down that night and slew 185,000 Assyrians and the city was saved.

Oh, we fume and fret and worry over our problems. But why not take them to the Lord and let Him solve them?

IV. WE PUT OUR SORROWS IN THE FOURTH WATERPOT AND RECEIVE COMFORT

If you haven't had a sorrow, you soon will have. The black camel kneels at every door. "Man is born unto trouble, as the sparks fly upward" (Job 5:7). "Man that is born of a woman is of few days, and full of trouble" (Job. 14:1). Yes, life is filled with sorrow and trouble. But listen to Psalm 55:22, "Cast thy burden upon the Lord, and he shall sustain thee: he shall never suffer the righteous to be moved." There's the answer. Bring Him your sorrows and you'll find comfort in Him.

Do you remember when that loved one passed away and how your heart was broken and how the tears fell? Where did you find comfort? Not in the things that you possessed. Not even in the words of your friends. No, you turned to God and He gave you the peace that passeth all understanding. You heard Him say, "Let not your heart be troubled, just trust in Me." Then your heart answered, "The Lord is my shepherd, I shall not want." And you found peace.

When I was a boy I heard Luther B. Bridgers preach. He was a Methodist evangelist. He was married and had two lovely daughters. They lived in Kentucky while he went over the country preaching in revivals. He was holding a meeting in Georgia when a message came, telling him that his home had burned down and that his wife and two daughters had perished in the fire. He went down into the depths of sorrow, but found Christ closer than ever before. Then he wrote a song, the chorus of which says:

Jesus, Jesus, Jesus —
Sweetest name I know,
Fills my every longing,
Keeps me singing as I go.

Yes, he brought his sorrows to Jesus and found comfort in Him. That's where we must find our comfort, also.

V. WE PUT OUR NEEDS IN THE FIFTH WATERPOT AND HE GIVES US HIS SUPPLY

"My God shall supply all your need according to his riches in glory by Christ Jesus" (Phil. 4:19). We have many needs, but God has everything and is ready to supply our needs.

Let me give you several Scriptures and you'll notice that in each one God promises to supply our needs, but He attaches a condition. There is something we must do before He will supply the need.

"No good thing will he withhold from them that walk uprightly" (Ps. 84:11). Note the condition is that we must walk uprightly,

"If ye abide in me, and my words abide in you, ye shall ask what ye will, and it shall be done unto you" (John 15:7).

"But seek ye first the kingdom of God, and his righteousness; and all these things shall be added unto you" (Matt. 6:33).

"Bring ye all the tithes into the storehouse, that there may be meat in mine house, and prove me now herewith, saith the Lord of hosts, if I will not open you the windows of heaven, and pour you out a blessing, that there shall not be room enough to receive it" (Mal. 3:10).

Note again the conditions with each promise. If we do our part, if we live rightly for Him, He will supply our every need. David said, "I have been young, and now am old; yet I have not seen the righteous forsaken, nor his seed begging bread" (Ps. 39:25). How true it is! Just live for Jesus and watch Him supply your needs.

VI. We Put Our Future in the Sixth Waterpot and He Gives Us Heaven

Oh, that's the sweetest wine, that's the best of it all. Wouldn't it hurt you to think that all you had waiting for you at the end was a cold grave and an everlasting hell? Well, that's all the unsaved man has to look forward to. But, thank God, in Christ we have a hope. We can trust Him for all the future and He will give us heaven.

I have known people who were sick, people who were sad, people who were broken-hearted, people who were poor. But they rested in one hope, that someday their trouble would be over and God would take them to heaven. A business man one cold and dreary morning bought a paper from a newsboy and said to him, "It's a rough day, isn't it?" And the boy smiled and said, "Yes, sir, but by and by, think of that." And the man thought of the springtime and the warm sunshine and flowers and his spirits were lifted.

Are you weary and heavy laden today? Well, by and by, think of that. God has something wonderful for you.

Heaven will be wonderful, not only because of the things that will be there, but because of the things that won't be there. We hunger here, but there'll be no hunger in heaven. We thirst here, but there'll be no thirst in heaven. We weep here, but there'll be no tears in heaven. We are in sorrow here, but there'll be no sorrow there. We have pain here, but there'll be no pain in heaven. Death comes here, but there are no graves on the hillside of glory. Instead of the hurtful things of this earth, we'll be in the presence of Christ, with all the wonderful things God has prepared for His children.

Just put your whole life in the hands of Jesus and He will give you back the richest blessings of this life and the bounties of the life to come.

Booth Tucker, the son-in-law of the founder of the Salvation Army, was preaching in the Salvation Hall in Chicago. As he spoke of God's grace he declared that this grace would be sufficient for every hour, every need. At the close of his message a man stood up and said, "Mr. Tucker, if your wife had just died and your children were crying for their mother, you couldn't say that God's grace was sufficient for every need." Mr. Tucker assured him that even under these circumstances he believed God's grace would sustain him.

The meeting ended and a few days later Booth Tucker's wife was killed in a railroad accident. They brought her body to that same Salvation Army hall for the funeral. Several preachers paid a glowing tribute to this fine Christian woman. At the close of the service Mr. Tucker asked to be allowed to say a few words. He stood with his hand on his wife's casket and said, "The other night when I was here a man stood up and said that God's grace would not be sufficient if my wife had just died and if the children were crying out for a mother that I could not bring back to them. But now my wife is gone and my little children cling to my fingers and cry out for their mother. My heart is breaking, but if that man is here I want to tell him that even now God's grace is sufficient. I have looked up to Him and He has sent peace and comfort to me, even in this sad hour."

The man was in the congregation when Mr. Tucker gave

his testimony and he came down to the front and said, "If Jesus Christ can do that for Booth Tucker, I want Him as my Saviour, too." And he gave his heart to Jesus and found salvation and peace.

Yes, every need can be satisfied in Jesus Christ. Come and fill these waterpots with all your needs and let Him turn them into sweetest wine.